Solo
Acoustic
Musician™
3
Booking a Gig

Michael Nichols

Solo Acoustic Musician 3: Booking A Gig

Copyright © 2023 by Michael Nichols

Printed in the United States of America

Paperback ISBN: 978-1-959096-78-8
eBook ISBN: 978-1-959096-79-5

Canoe Tree
Press

4697 Main Street
Manchester Center, VT 05255

Canoe Tree Press is a division of DartFrog Books

TABLE OF CONTENTS

 # DEFINITION OF A SOLO ACOUSTIC MUSICIAN

Solo: Done by one person alone; unaccompanied.

Acoustic: Relating to sound or the sense of hearing. When referring to popular music or musical instruments, not employing electrical amplification.

Musician: A person who plays a musical instrument, especially as a profession, or is musically talented.

My definition of a Solo Acoustic Musician (SAM in the pages that follow) is straightforward: one person with an acoustic instrument, performing songs with or without vocals, hopefully for an audience.

There is something intrinsically pure about a person making music and singing songs with an acoustic instrument. To me, that's what a Solo Acoustic Musician is, and it's one of the most original forms of musical expression.

A SOLO ACOUSTIC MUSICIAN'S CODE OF CONDUCT

Always be on time.

Dress appropriately for the gig.

Don't get drunk onstage or in the venue.

Clean up after yourself at the end of your gig.

Promote your music and your gigs.

Network with other musicians.

Use your gifts and talents to help others.

Show respect to yourself and others by not engaging in lewd language on the microphone.

Represent yourself, the agents, and the clients as best you can by being professional on the gig.

 **INTRODUCTION**

In this third volume of the Solo Acoustic Musician series, I want to shine a light on the perspectives of the people who hire SAMs to play music in their venues. I intend to provide useful insights into what managers, owners, and agents think when it comes to booking musicians. As a Solo Acoustic Musician, I have worked with many kinds of people over the years, and I thought it would be valuable to interview some of them and share those conversations with the reader, offering an inside look at what the people who pay us to perform have to say about us and what they think. I hope that we can learn more about what we need to do to book gigs and build relationships with the people who handle the calendars for the venues in which we play our music.

After interviewing other Solo Acoustic Musicians in SAM 2, I thought it would be a natural next step to conduct more interviews. I had a lot of fun hanging out with other musicians and learning about their lives and experiences as gigging musicians. When I decided to interview the people that book us to play our gigs, I knew I would need to up my game a little. The SAM 2 interviews were pretty casual, though I did have a checklist of subjects to discuss based on the chapters and subchapters from SAM 1. For this book, I knew that I needed to become a little more serious about my preparation and time management. The people I have chosen to interview in this book are busy people with a lot going on, and I wanted to be well-prepared for each interview.

In SAM 1, the chapter with the highest word count was the chapter about booking gigs. SAM 3 is basically an expansion of that chapter. I have added more of my opinions on how to book a gig. I have also shared some stories from my own life and career as well. Diving into the conversations with the people who are in charge of venue calendars should open your eyes to the business side of this lifestyle.

Once you have spent time developing your instrumental skills and your singing voice, it will be time to book a gig. I think it is very important to know what is going on in the mind of the person who is going to hire you. Having some examples of what they are looking for and expecting of you is crucial to becoming a master at booking yourself and making a living as a Solo Acoustic Musician.

I am going to outline a basic checklist for you to use to ask questions and fill in the answers that you receive from, each prospective client. Organizing your sales pitch and knowing what you need to ask of the venue representative is vital to be on top of your game when booking gigs. It can be hard to remember all the details, and making notes and organizing them in a file so that you can quickly and easily reference the information is crucial to your success.

# PERSONAL UPDATES

In SAM 2, I made a list of personal updates that went along with the order of the chapters in SAM 1. I am going to take a different approach to how I share updates with you this time. Here we go...

Every year I have a small list of goals that include filling my calendar with gigs, making more money, and learning songs. In the past I've also had categories like writing original songs, making a CD (that would include recording, mixing, mastering, packaging, and releasing), and upgrading my equipment. I'll be honest, I still haven't bought a new guitar. I think I'm just so used to my guitar that I can't find one I like, but that's a whole other story.

My focus today is to tell you about my goal of learning 300 songs for the year 2022. I'm writing this on December 28, and I'm at 279 songs. I don't think I'm going to force myself to try to squeeze in another 21 songs by the end of this year. I might learn a few more, but I'm not going to go nuts about making it to 300. I feel very satisfied, even though I didn't actually hit the specific number 300, because I made a lot of progress. The overall goal was to learn a lot of new songs and increase the diversity of my repertoire. I have definitely accomplished this task. I've always learned a lot of songs, but I've never kept track of how many before and I wanted to know the number during a specific period of time. I tracked that information on my monthly calendar, writing a number at the end of each week. I also added a category to my yearly spreadsheet so that I can see the total along with my financial information.

Believe it or not, it is not easy to learn 300 songs in a year. I think it has really made me stretch my comfort zone, and I even found some new comfort zones. I decided to give in and learn songs I never really wanted to play, stepping outside the box to work on styles of music that I'm not used to playing. Let me tell you about some of what I'm talking about.

I grew up in the '80s when hair metal bands were really popular, but I never learned "Every Rose Has Its Thorn" by the band Poison. I have to tell you that I sing and play it well, and every time I do, people sing along and really enjoy it. It was worth the effort and it's fun to play. I never wanted to learn "Wonderwall" by the band Oasis; for years, I would avoid it at all costs, but some fans that regularly come to see me play have been asking me to do it for a long time. I finally learned it and they went crazy. They sang along to every word and tipped me a whole bunch of money, so whenever they come around I play it for them. I've actually played that song out at a gig about five times now, but only for those people. I have not actually picked it out myself to throw into the mix on just any gig yet, but if someone comes up and requests that song, I know that I can play it successfully now. My one hope is that it makes me some tips if somebody does request it.

A similar song to "Wonderwall" is "Wagon Wheel" by Bob Dylan and Ketch Secor, which had been requested a lot over the last four or five years, and now I know how to play it and it's in my songbook. I think I've played it five or six times and the people were so happy that I played it for them that it made it worth it for me to have it on standby. A fun thing about this song is that when I started reading the lyrics, I realized that I had played music in every geographic location listed in the song with the exception of the Cumberland Gap near Johnson City, Tennessee. I didn't really like this song, but now that I know the words, it has become special to me and it stimulates memories of my travels and gigs from long ago. I learned a lot of songs this past year for other people, but I also picked out a bunch of songs that I wanted to learn how to play and sing for myself and my own enjoyment.

I've come to the conclusion that I'm in the "quantity over quality" part of the process and that probably 10% of the songs I've learned this year I don't really play that well yet. I will need a little more practice, and that's okay; I don't feel bad about putting them in my songbook. But on the opposite end of that spectrum, there are at least 30 songs that I took to very quickly and I play very well. That leaves a big chunk of songs that are probably just good enough, and that's fine with me as well. During the last year, I've learned about a bunch of new musicians I've never heard of before and that was exciting. I have been more accepting of trying new things when it comes to picking out songs on my own.

I learned "I've Been Everywhere" by Johnny Cash, and I even wrote two new verses and I plan to write three more. I wrote a verse for my state of Florida and also for the county where I live. I play gigs in the three counties that surround mine on a regular basis and I plan to write verses for each one of them as well. I learned "Time" and "Breathe" by Pink Floyd, and I medley them together and use my loop pedal to build a beautiful full-band sound that people are responding to in an awesome way. For months I would wake up and look forward to going to work to play the song "Breathe," because it was just so different and so much fun and people responded in such a positive way. I don't think I had felt like that about a specific song for years. During this past year, I have found myself feeling like that about several different songs and it's quite exciting for me.

Even though I had been learning a lot of songs all the time over these years, it's still very easy to get into a rut and with the number of gigs I play, I can sometimes feel blah about going to work. It's nice to hit the refresh button sometimes, and some of these songs really do add something to my own personal experience when I'm performing. I get a lot of people coming up to me telling me they're tired of hearing Solo Acoustic Musicians play "Wish You Were Here" and "Comfortably Numb." They tell me it's refreshing to hear something different by Pink Floyd.

The music business doesn't take up that much of my time. I probably should put a little more energy into it.
—Alan Jackson

Another song that people are telling me is refreshing is "You Wreck Me" by Tom Petty. People in the audience at restaurants and bars are pretty tired of hearing "Free Fallin'" and "Last Dance With Mary Jane," so I am getting a ton of good feedback by adding some other Tom Petty songs to my list. Plus I'm having a lot of fun playing them. I added "What a Wonderful World" by Louis Armstrong to my songbook, and I use my mouth to play a trumpet solo. When I pretend to play the trumpet it turns people's heads and gets some attention from the audience which is good. There have even been a few times when people clapped for my "trumpet solo," which made me feel like I did a good job that day. These are just a few examples of the songs that I learned this year that I like to pull out and have a lot of fun playing.

In the OnSong app I use on my iPad I have a master list of all my songs and I also have the ability to make books. So I decided to assemble books based on genre or era. I have also added some books based on the number of songs I know by a certain artist. I know almost 20 Tom Petty songs, so I made a book just for him and the same is true of Bob Marley and a handful of other artists or bands. Doing this makes it easy and quick if someone asks for a specific musician; I can just go right to a list of only their songs.

Examples:

By Decade or Era

The '50s-'60s, '70s, '80s, '90s, 2000s, 2010s, & 2020s

By Genre

Rock, Reggae, Blues, Country, ALF, Comedy/Adult Content, and Loops

Another tactic I applied when I was trying to find songs to learn was looking at my various books and seeing which ones were deficient in number. I noticed right away that the 2000s, 2010s, and 2020s needed more songs. As I cross-referenced that with, for example, Country, I knew right away I needed some newer country songs in my songbook. I also applied this to the ALF book and beefed up my selection of songs that I thought would be appropriate for those venues.

My most productive month was May when I learned fifty-five songs, and my least productive month was June when I learned just seven songs. I am going to learn new songs in 2023, but I think I'm going to set a goal of 52. I will probably learn 100, but I'm not going to push myself like I did this past year. My main goal for 2023 is to improve my guitar skills and try to find some songs that will really showcase my playing. Some of the songs I'm thinking of learning this year may take a week or a month to get right, but they will be impressive and in my mind showstoppers or a big deal. If I can add 10 songs like that to my songbook, that will be massive. I am also going to go back through my songbook and learn some more signature riffs for the songs that are already there, and even learn a few note-for-note solos on certain songs. I will also spend a little time tidying up what I learned this past year by practicing and fixing a few of the songs that aren't going so well.

I am an experienced guitar player, but I don't know everything I could, and I'm going to use online sources like YouTube to push myself to improve my skills this year and take it up a notch. Improving my guitar playing will show up in my live gigs and it will help me demonstrate another level of value to the venue, as well as gain more attention from the audience.

Wish me luck on my journey, and I hope you set some new goals for yourself as well.

 # GUITAR PICK IN MY SHOE

I usually carry two, three, or even four picks in my pocket most every day of my life, and definitely 100% of the time when I'm going to a gig. Last month on a chilly night I wore pants to a gig, and I hadn't worn this particular pair of pants since the previous winter. Since I hadn't worn them in such a long time, I totally forgot about the hole in one of the pockets.

Now let's jump ahead to the next day when I had two gigs. One of them was in the afternoon with a one o'clock start time. I parked two blocks away, near where my evening gig was located, and I walked down the street with my cart to the first gig of the day. At some point, while I was setting up, I felt like there was something in my shoe. Maybe it could be a little stick or a little rock or something. So like any normal person, I took off my shoe to shake out whatever was in my shoe. Out onto the floor fell a guitar pick. One of the bartenders was walking by and remarked to me that I must be a professional musician to have guitar picks falling out of my shoes. I smiled and kind of giggled because it was funny.

When I got home the night before and put the contents of my pockets on the table, as I always do out of habit, I thought I was missing a pick, but it's so hard to keep track of all those guitar picks. I admit that just about the time I think I've seen and experienced everything, some new little thing will happen. This is the first time I've ever found a guitar pick in my shoe. As we all know, it's a running joke with guitar players that picks get everywhere, and I have found them in some pretty odd places, but never in my shoe until now. (I pulled out the sewing kit and fixed the pocket in those pants.)

AUDIENCE MISTAKE CLAP

As a Solo Acoustic Musician, I am playing the music by myself and there is no drumbeat. Something that sometimes happens in the middle of a song is if I stop playing the guitar, people think it's the end and they start to clap. One of my favorite musical words is "dynamics"; as songs build up to a climax and come back down, sometimes there's a pause in the music. This pause can include both a stop in the guitar and the vocals, and I have noticed over the years that this can trigger people to think it's the end of the song and they'll start to clap. Then when I start playing again, they feel a little silly and it's kind of a weird vibe sometimes. A lot of the time, at the end of that song, they won't clap at all because of the mistake they made earlier.

Something I try to do now when I know that a pause like that is coming is to try to do something to let them know that it's not the end of the song. One thing we do as cover musicians, meaning playing other people's songs, is that we try to play the song as it was done by the original artist. But there are times when we try to make the song our own and we adjust the arrangement or the key, rhythm, or tempo to fit our own personal style or way of doing things. If I can hold out a sustained chord, tap on my guitar to count out beats, or maybe even just play the rhythm through what should have been a break, then I can avoid that awkward moment when an audience member claps and it's not the end of the song. In a busy restaurant or bar environment, people are listening, but it's not the main thing they are focused on, so when the music stops for any reason, they tend to start clapping.

Personally, I love to drop completely drop out and come back in as part of the dynamic build-up and beautiful resolution part of a song. But I find it confuses people, so it's better to just fill that space with some kind of noise, music, or singing. When people see a full band play, they don't clap during quiet moments, because the end is signaled by the drummer, and it's easier to tell that it's the end of the song.

DO ONE THING EVERY DAY

First of all, I have to give some credit to a fan who was messaging back and forth with me on social media. I am thankful for a reminder of something I used to tell other musicians all the time. The simple task of doing one thing every day for your music career should not be overlooked or forgotten. I used to say that it's kind of like making a small snowball and pushing it down a hill. It will gather more momentum and get bigger and bigger as it goes. Just a little bit at a time, but it gets bigger and stronger while picking up speed and momentum.

My standard practice for all these years has been to do at least one thing every day for my music career. There are advantages today that I didn't have when I started, so I would raise the number to five things or even ten things every day. With the use of social media, it is very easy to make a post and thank your fans for coming out to your gig last night or send a note to the bar or manager who booked you and say thank you to them as well.

For the music business, social networking is brilliant.
Just when you think it's doom and gloom and you have
to spend millions of pounds on marketing and this
and that, you have this amazing thing now called fan
power. The whole world is linked through a laptop. It's
amazing. And it's free. I love it. It's absolutely brilliant.
—Simon Cowell

You could do both of those things quickly and easily. So you can see how it can add up very fast and quickly become more than one thing every day. But the old standard of one thing every day is solid.

I remember having conversations with other musicians who would ask me, "Yeah, but what about Christmas or Thanksgiving? Do you ever skip a day or take a day off?" My previous two examples are good for this. Reaching out and thanking someone who has booked you at their venue or a fan or group of fans who have come out to your shows is actually appropriate on a holiday. Both of those count as doing a thing for your career. I will say that you don't want to call someone to try to book a gig on a holiday. Make a note of that because it is bad etiquette.

There are a lot of examples of things you can do to further your career in the music business. As a Solo Acoustic Musician, you can practice your guitar. You can learn a new guitar chord or a new inversion of a chord you already know. You can learn a new song. You can organize your song list in your songbook or iPad. You can put on new strings. You can make a new contact. You can record a song. You can promote a gig. The list is quite long and maybe even endless. There are a lot of things you can do to further your musical endeavors. Even on a holiday when you don't want to send out sales pitches, you can just work on your sales pitch and try to make it better. The one or two-paragraph sales pitch that you develop can be an ongoing endeavor.

I think you get the idea, and you can see that it would be pretty easy to do more than one thing every day that will help you build your future. You could even make a list of categories and then try to do one thing in each category every day. Let's just start with a few basics like playing your guitar, learning a song, and trying to book a gig. Maybe you practice your guitar for thirty minutes and then after that, you get halfway through learning a new song. That will add up if you do it every day for a whole month. You will have practiced your guitar for many hours, and you will probably have added five or six new songs to your song list. Maybe more, maybe less, but you'll be further ahead than you were at the beginning of the month. If you multiply that by twelve months, you will see a lot of results. A big part of this is developing consistency.

In life, progress is a measure of success. If you are consistently making forward progress in a direction that improves your life, then you are being successful. Each small goal leads to the achievement of another, and so on until you have realized a larger goal on your list. There are lots of motivational sayings about this subject, so I won't bore you with repetitious quotes that somebody else coined. I will say that you can achieve a successful, consistent musical career and it can start with the simple concept of making sure you do at least one thing towards your goal every day.

When you are trying to book a gig, maybe you will talk to ten new potential clients. If you made one phone call or email every day for a month, then that would be thirty people contacted. Hopefully, you actually speak to someone or get a response to an email from ten of them. Maybe you got two new gigs out of all that effort. But if you multiply that times twelve months, that would be twenty-four new clients in one year. With luck, those become residual clients and you get to be in the venue's rotation and play there more than once. Just by simply doing one thing every day, it grows over time.

The other day I was running errands and I didn't have to go out of my way to stop at a restaurant and talk to someone about a gig. I decided to stop at a bar along my route. I was lucky that day and the manager who does the booking was on site. We got to chat a little bit and I was able to get a date on the calendar. It only took me about five minutes. I could have very easily talked myself out of stopping there at that time, but I challenged myself to just go inside the place and see what happened. Even if that was the only thing I did for my music career that day, it was a success. I now have a new client and have filled an empty spot on my calendar. If I do a good job on the gig, then I will get more dates on my calendar at that venue and have a new residual client to book gigs with in the future. By not giving up or making an excuse to not stop, I may have added thousands of dollars to my calendar. I really had no reason to delay or hold back, and my attempt paid off.

On my list of things to do today, and because it's a Saturday, is to work on a new song. As I talked about in the first book, I don't like to call or email people about bookings on a Saturday because it's one of the busiest days in any restaurant or bar. So while I have a little time here at the house, I'm going to work on a new song. Of course, on Monday I'm going to call two or three restaurants or bars about booking a gig.

Doing one thing or more things every day requires consistency and balance. It takes a little bit of follow-through to just do something and if you do follow through, you will make something happen. Even on a day when you feel lazy, you can find one thing to do for your musical journey. Put the idea into practice and see how it develops over a month or two. When it comes to your goals, I promise that you will be farther ahead than you were before you started.

Since this book includes interviews with managers, owners, and agents that book us on their calendars, make one of your categories something to do with them. A daily attempt at connecting with a new venue representative would be a challenge. By making some phone calls and sending some emails every day, I think you could find yourself with quite a few new gigs on the calendar. It takes a lot of effort to keep a calendar full of gigs, and you don't want to procrastinate. Trying to catch up last minute and having an empty or a half-full calendar is stressful. Stay ahead of the situation by doing at least one thing every day.

I have just given you a challenge. Do you accept?

If you do accept my challenge, then put the book down right now and look up a bar or restaurant that you want to play and call them or send them an email with your sales pitch. If you are not ready right this moment because you want to apply more of the information in this book to refine your sales pitch, then make a note on your to-do list. Doing this will ensure that you will not put it off any longer than you have to by proceeding to make that call immediately after finishing this book.

Reading this page does not count as doing one thing today. LOL

I find that if I get started doing anything toward my goal, I often end up doing more. For example, if I plan, schedule, or force myself to play or practice my guitar for five to ten minutes, I will end up playing for a lot longer and find myself making more gains in the direction of my goals. It is the same with planning my phone calls, looking up venues, and organizing my files or venue information. It just always seems that as long as I get started and I have convinced myself to do at least one thing, I end up doing more.

Contacting venue representatives gets easier the more I do it. I have less anxiety and become more confident if I just get started and make a call. I think it is totally understandable to feel nervous and stressed when I am thinking about calling a stranger and asking them for money to come play music in their bar, but I don't want it to overwhelm me and I won't allow myself to be ruled by fear. So what if they don't hire me? I am just going to call another place. I find that as long as I do the one thing I put on my clipboard, I will actually want to do more, and I will follow through. Just like I learn songs in batches, I will contact many venues in a row when I am in the mood to sell myself. It's funny how the energy shift happens when you just get over the hump and pick up the phone. The immediate gratification of booking a gig on a first phone call is totally exhilarating.

If I do not hold myself accountable, and I skip a day, I don't feel good. I know I am supposed to make an effort to do at least one thing every day, even a small thing. My personal responsibility to my music and my business is mine alone and not only is no one else going to do any of it for me, no one else can.

Make a list of the places you've called. Don't just flip pages in the phone book or scroll down a website listing live music venues and jump around willy-nilly. Organize yourself and write down the name of each venue you've contacted (by phone or email). When you are done each day, you will be able to see your progress and when you start the next day you will know where to begin.

Do you have a local entertainment newspaper like City Paper or Creative Loafing? Maybe that, or a website listing local events, is something you can look at. You can cold call right down that list if you want to.

I will be honest — sometimes I just think I am going to make my one thing for the day the organizing of my desk and all the pieces of paper that clutter it up. All these notes about songs to learn and venues to call get piled up near my computer and sometimes I have to force myself to clean it up and do something about it. What do you think happens once I get started on that project? If you said that I get energized and actually spend more time working on the things that I have written on all those pieces of paper, you would be correct. I become reminded of people I wanted to call and songs I wanted to learn and I just get going. It always feels better once I have cleaned things up, overcome my procrastination, and moved closer to where I want to be in life. On really good days, I will have added a couple of songs to my songbook while simultaneously adding a few dates to my calendar, all while neatly organizing my workspace.

There ain't no tomorrow quite as nice as today.
—Unknown

Finding reminders on my desk and doing something about them always feels good. It doesn't matter how big or how small the task on the reminder note is. It hasn't been removed from my desk because I have not yet done anything about it. The more of them that pile up, the harder it can be to get started, and that can become the one thing I need to do each day. Just get started and the rest will follow.

The smile that the bartender gets because I finally learned a song she wanted me to play is my motivation. When a regular customer at one of my usual venues comes to see me play and I have learned the Rolling Stones song that he wanted to hear, it makes him happy and I share in that happiness. If you ever need more motivation other than your personal desire for success to do one thing toward your musical goals every day, think of the audience.

I thought to myself, I wonder if the person reading this book believes that I practice what I preach, so I stopped typing and took action in a different way. I looked up assisted living facilities in my county. I found a database with more than a hundred locations and decided to call one. I ended up calling six because every conversation I had was delightful and easy. I obtained contact information for the activity director at every location I called. I had heard of these gigs before, but I didn't know there were so many and I didn't know that evidently, they all have some form of a music program. I have just opened up a huge resource that I had never explored before, and it was easy. It will become a new gig category for my calendar. My one thing turned into six today and will become more tomorrow. On top of that, I am confident in my promo videos, my abilities, and my chances of getting gigs from the emails I sent out today. It all started by doing just one thing toward my goal.

It feels good to do one thing every day.

 # BY THE NUMBERS

As with many types of sales jobs, our mission is to reach out to as many potential clients as possible. If I call or email one hundred venues trying to book gigs, there is a good chance that I will get some shows on my calendar. It would be safe to say that if I call two hundred venues, the number of gigs that I book will increase. It can totally be a numbers game and the more venues you contact, the better odds you have of filling your calendar. Maybe my numbers of one hundred and two hundred aren't realistic for where you live, but I hope you get the idea. If you only try to work with one venue, then you are severely limiting your chances of having a full calendar. Even if you have to reach out a little further on your map and book gigs in a town an hour away, it will be beneficial to grow your business contacts list to include those venues. Using the venue list in SAM 2 can also help you get more creative with venues nearby that you may not have thought of before. The point is to try to develop as many potential clients as you can over time. You can even set a weekly goal of approaching two new venues every week. After one year you will have contacted more than one hundred venues and with a little luck, you should have booked gigs with a percentage of these potential clients. It can be fun, and you can treat it like a game where you try to improve your skills and learn from your mistakes as you advance in levels.

There have been times when I booked a gig with a new client on the first phone call. A paid gig on my calendar with just my spoken word sales pitch on the phone. No promo video. No demo music. No email or manila envelope was involved. Sometimes all it takes is a good sales pitch and a little luck. I found that the more calls I made, the better I became at selling myself. Of course, I had bad calls along the way, and I also had to make many follow-up calls. I remember more than one venue that took me years to get a date booked. I was persistent and I did not give up easily.

This concept of By the Numbers is based on statistics and probabilities. If you can call 100 places and get 10 gigs, that is a 10% success rate. If you have a good sales pitch, maybe you get 17 gigs or even 27. The point of the by-the-numbers idea is that you only get one gig if you call one venue, and that's not a guarantee now because you might get turned down by that one place. The part of our lifestyle that is sales can be overwhelming, so the more you embrace it and try to get comfortable making your pitch to many types of venues and representatives, the better off you are going to be in the future.

If you make 0 phone calls or emails, then you get 0 gigs.

If you make one phone call or send one email, you might get 1 gig.

If you make 20 phone calls and emails, you might get 4 gigs.

If you make 200 phone calls and emails, you might get 40 gigs.

That is actually a pretty high percentage rate unless your sales pitch is really good, but I say it for effect.

All of those gigs could become clients that you work with for years. Some of them might just be one-offs. If you play it by the numbers, then you also know that it's a continuous thing that you have to do by making more phone calls and sending more emails basically forever.

It's a reality that I know and I live by. In the past, I've also known musicians who got tired of it and didn't want to do it anymore, only to go get themselves a job doing sales for some other product that they found easier to sell than themselves. I have my own opinions about that, but that's a topic for another time.

Those musicians chose to sell steaks door to door, cars on a used car lot, or cable and internet services, and they weren't focused on being full-time Solo Acoustic Musicians. The point is, it was still the same amount of work, if not more, and it was still by the numbers because in order to sell steaks door-to-door you have to knock on a lot of doors. If you want to sell cars on a used car lot, then you better get people on that lot, and you better talk to a lot of people. Lastly, if you want to cold call or go door-to-door to sell cable TV and internet services, then you better go talk to about 1000 people every week. (I'm just guessing about some of these numbers because I don't know from experience. I just know what I have heard people say around the way. I call it the word on the street.)

I just find it easier to sell myself, playing my guitar and singing. I'm confident in my abilities and myself as a product, and every person I talk to is a potential client. One of the reasons I chose to live where I do is that there is a lot of work for musicians, and a lot of venues that hire guys like me, so I have no shortage of places to call or email or actually visit and talk to someone.

Keep track of what you do. Call and talk to as many people as you can. Send out as many emails with your promo video as you can until you fill your calendar.

Do it by the numbers.

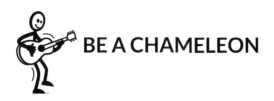 # BE A CHAMELEON

Over time, you are going to be meeting and talking with a lot of different people. The ability to be flexible and adjust your sales pitches on the fly will be very beneficial. In my experience, I have had to pitch every type of person I can imagine. Some people are very casual about the music booking for their restaurant and of course, some people are the complete opposite and can be very uptight and particular with running their calendar. Every venue has a different budget and concept for the entertainment they want to spend that money on.

It can be very important to try to understand to whom you are selling your services. Sometimes I will go to a venue and scout out the room. What I mean is that I will come in like a customer and blend in with the crowd. I won't approach any employees about music booking. I will have a snack or get something to drink and check out the vibe of the room. I may decide that I don't want to play music there, or I may decide to call them the next day and ask for the person in charge of booking live music.

I have been out "gig fishing" or "venue scouting" and have been sitting at a bar with a beer and an appetizer, only to see a manager yell at multiple employees and treat people poorly. I immediately think there is a possibility this is how that person could interact with me. Do I want to put up with that? Am I willing to take the chance? Like a lot of abusive relationships, it would probably start off happily — they would be nice to me, book me, and pay me. I'd play there a few times and then one day they would have a bad day and for some reason, I would be the one that they would turn their attention to and start treating me poorly. It's an observation I've made many times, and over the years I have actually tested this theory.

To put things in context, my calendar is always full. So if I go to a gig and the manager or venue representative decides to be a complete jerk to me, then I'm usually in a position to just pack up and leave, because I don't have to put up with that kind of treatment. I think I've even told a couple of stories in the previous two books where I made it clear that it's not acceptable in my world and it shouldn't be in yours either.

Technology has opened up the music business 100-fold and provided space for all kinds of new faces.
—Andy Mineo

Some people would interpret being a chameleon as being a people-pleaser, and that may be part of it, but that is not really what I'm talking about. If you are so rigid in your sales pitch and your approach to booking gigs that you don't get any takers, then you might want to loosen it up a little bit and try to blend in with what's going on. I know Solo Acoustic Musicians who only play country or only play blues, and this limits their options based on what venues in their location book that style or genre of music. But what I'm talking about more specifically right now is personal relationship communication development, which deals with a possibility of an unknown amount of potential residual clients. I may encounter, call, or email ten new potential residual clients and they will all be different kinds of people. I could do that once a month throughout the year, encountering 120 different personalities. That can be an overwhelming number of different personalities to try to sell yourself to.

Think about mixed martial arts; it's good to know a little bit about all the different styles when you get in the ring to fight someone who might know all of them as well. Just like learning different styles of music, there are different styles of communication. There are different lifestyles of individuals and although you have to be strong and committed to who you are it's probably best that you are flexible, especially when you are trying to sell yourself to these different individuals. If you came at everybody with the same sales pitch and there was no individuality, then it would probably seem like a copy-and-paste approach.

Start by personalizing your pitches. Adding someone's name and/or the venue's name to an email makes it stand out a little bit. You want them to know who you are or remember you, and hopefully, your sales pitch paragraph along with your promo video as well, but it definitely doesn't hurt to address them directly.

Each sales pitch is important, and although you may be sending out twenty emails in one day, you need to take the time to make sure that each of them has a little bit of personal detail. When I get going, it can feel like an assembly line of sales pitches: emails backed up with phone calls and more sales pitches. It can be really easy to move too fast and send an email to somebody with someone else's name on it. This may seem like common sense, but if you copy and paste a previous email and send it to someone with the previous contact person's name on it, you have just shut yourself out of a gig. Don't make this mistake and negate your good intentions. Take a minute to double-check to whom you have addressed your message before sending it.

I know for a fact that somebody reading this book right now is making a face and thinking, that would never happen to me because I'm so cool. Six months or a year from now, they will end up sending someone an email and never getting a response because they put Frank instead of John. Something that small can alienate a potential client and cost you years of income.

Most people only know one thing about chameleons, and that's that they change color to blend in with their environment as a defense mechanism. I don't know a lot about them, but I'm pretty sure they don't move very fast. The point I'm making is that sometimes it's better to just slow down for a minute and double-check your work. Make sure that you are sending the email to the right person. I hope I have saved you the embarrassment of trying to apologize your way out of that debacle because it's a tough one to get out of in any circumstance.

Although I might not be able to drive and visit everywhere on my list of potential clients, by looking at their website and social media pages I can get quite a good bit of information. I don't think I will get as much information as I would in person, but it is still better than doing no homework at all. Learning about the environment, the ambiance, and the menus can help me tailor my sales pitch for each venue. It can give me an idea about their customer base and who I would be playing music for, as well as what kind of wardrobe might be appropriate to wear when I am there in person.

Like a chameleon, I may need to adjust myself to blend in with the surroundings and fit in with the vibe of the venue. The same is true with how I might choose to communicate with the venue representative in charge of booking live music. We have to be true to ourselves, and I am not suggesting that you create a fake persona for the purpose of booking gigs. But being flexible and adapting to different clients will be a valuable skill set to develop.

LEARN WHAT KIND OF VENUES WORK FOR YOU

There are times when I play in a new venue and it goes really well and I look forward to returning again for another gig. The exact opposite happens as well; sometimes after I play a place, I do not ever want to go back. There are many different types of venues and there are many different people I have to deal with to book myself in those venues. Sometimes these parts of the equation work for me and sometimes they do not. I have tried to develop my own sense of when things are working and when they are not going well.

- What style of music do you play?

- What kind of places do you want to perform your music?

- Is there a specific kind of venue that you prefer?

In SAM 2, I made a list of types of venues and I know Solo Acoustic Musicians who could book and play gigs in any of them while at the same time, I know SAMs who only play blues or country music which might limit them to only certain types of venues. Being musically versatile is clearly an advantage to booking gigs in many different types of venues. But developing your sales pitch is important also, because if you only play blues or country as in my previous example, then you could pitch a blues night or country night to a venue that typically wouldn't normally book those types of musicians.

The more you are able to add variety to your musical mix, your wardrobe, and your overall vibe, the more types of venues you will be able to add in your pursuit of booking gigs.

I sometimes like a certain type of venue, only to have a specific place not work out for me. I may like to play at yacht clubs, but have had a bad experience at a specific one and do not want to play there again. I may have the same type of experience where I enjoy playing at one sports bar and then do not enjoy playing at another. Sometimes it could be the interaction with the venue representative that makes the difference. I like the saying that it's "par for the course," but sometimes the course is the same but different. I have come across many examples of what works for me and by making notes about every aspect of a gig and a venue type, I am able to compare all the different examples.

The venues that work best for me are ones where the employees treat me nicely and with respect while I encounter receptive audiences who treat me the same way. There are many variables that can change these ideal experiences, but they are usually overshadowed by the good things so it is almost always balanced in my favor.

When you start to learn about what venues work for you, it will probably involve you making a list of things you want.

- Is there a stage?
- Type of music?
- Pay scale?
- Hours of playing?
- Etc.

A good way to learn what kind of venue works for you is to make a list of what you want and then, when you initiate contact with the venue representative, you will have questions that need answers or categories that need to be checked off before you decide to play there.

I think the path is different for everybody. Go after the doors that are open to you. That has always been my motto for getting into the music business. Do the things that seem to be good opportunities and work hard at them. Try to make good decisions and be nice. Hopefully, all of that will pay off at some point.
—Chris Stapleton

I have frequently gone to bars and restaurants in an incognito way. I pretend that I am "undercover," just to see if I want to play there or if I think it would be good for me to play music there. I have seen owners and managers berate customers and employees during a busy dinner service. That's when I thought, "Wow! They could talk to me like that, and I don't think that I want to play music in that environment." It can be just that quick. On the opposite end of things, I sometimes make a call and get a gig and the first time that I am in the venue is when I arrive to load in and set up. Of course, I hope it goes well, but sometimes it doesn't, and that is a part of life.

When I was younger, I wasn't picky about where I played at all. I also put up with being treated poorly all the time. As I have grown older and become more mature, I have come to know my own worth. I also understand how I should be treated, and I have the confidence to walk away from a venue where I don't feel it is a good fit. I find that if my musical style matches the venue, that is only one part of what works for me. I also want to make a certain amount of money and be treated fairly by the staff. If you have read SAM 1 and SAM 2, then you know that I want a safe place to play where the weather will not ruin my equipment.

I still like to rock out in a loud aggressive way like I did when I was younger. But I don't want to do that five nights a week anymore. I used to stand and move around a lot more, and now I find that I like to sit some nights and be relaxed while I play. I find that for me, a balance of different venues works. I like to have a few quiet restaurants where I can sit and play a certain way that is low volume and mellow. I balance that out by having an active tiki or dive bar to play in where I can turn up the volume and stomp my feet. I enjoy playing a mix of adult content and comedy songs, and I have at least one venue a month where I get to do those sets. Having different types of venues allows me to express myself in different ways and keeps me fresh and engaged in my own musical world.

I hope you can find venues that work for you.

 **BUSINESS CARDS**

I know we all probably have our own business cards by now, but it is still an important topic to discuss. The basics should be on your business card: your name, phone number, and your email address should be on the front. You could also add your website address. I have added a QR code on the back of my card and if you scan it, it will take you directly to my website.

There is something that happens during the exchange of business cards, and I call it the business card dance. It happens like this... I give someone my business card and say something like, "Call me" or "Text me." This is followed by them saying "Here's my card," and handing me their card. This interaction has always confused me. It doesn't just happen in business because this scenario has played out in my personal life as well.

I keep business cards in my little beach bag. One reason that I do this is that they make good bookmarks when I am reading. The other reason is that if I get to talking with someone on the beach, I can grab a card from my bag and hand it to them. A month ago, when I was at the beach, I gave my card to someone I had talked with many times. I followed it up by telling them to call or text me so we could stay in touch and coordinate with our other beach friends during the winter months. Then he went out of his way to walk all the way out into the parking lot and retrieve his own business card from his vehicle, handing it to me and telling me to call him. I have to admit that I am over this response in my personal life. Here we are more than a month later and I have not received a call or text from him. I have not sent him one, either.

In business, I am selling my musical products and services, so I will adjust and bend to making the first move by sending a message or making a call. But when it comes to my personal life and I give someone my card or email them my number and request that they call me, I will not reply if they just give me their number in response. I think it is rude. The guy on the beach could have just texted me right there while we were talking, but instead chose to go all the way to his car and get his card. We have a group of mutual beach friends and I have all of their numbers except for his, which I find humorous. Why did he respond like that?

I think probably my main advice to new artists is if you want to be in the music business, you need to be dang serious about it because it's a rough business.
—Leon Russell

The same thing happens with emails. I will send an email and ask someone to call me when they are ready to talk. They will respond by sending me their number. I think that this is a weird situation. What I have figured out is that this response is a psychological (conscious or subconscious) tactic to "control the frame." Now that is a deep subject to discuss, and there are whole books out there about it. I will try to explain what I mean without going too far into it. Controlling the frame is a tactic to retain control of the situation. If I give you my number and you call me, then I control the frame and the situation. You have called me and want or need something from me. I hope you get what I am saying.

I have had many conversations with other Solo Acoustic Musicians over the years and a common theme I hear repeated is how the venue representative has not called. They will say to me that they have dropped off a card three or four times and the person in charge of booking has not called them yet. My advice is always the same. Get *their* card and contact *them*. It's that easy, and the best thing that you can do. While they are in control of the frame, the best thing for you to do is to initiate contact. You want something from them, and it is your job to make the first move.

I have told you stories and provided examples of how it has taken me years to get a response or get a gig at a certain venue. If you drop off a card and don't get their information, you have basically done nothing. It is always good to leave a card for them, so don't get me wrong, keep doing that. But it cannot and should not be the only thing you do to get their attention.

When I go "gig fishing," I always leave my card but the thing I want to make sure I do every time is to get the contact information of the venue representative. I want to be able to send them an email with my promo video and my sales pitch. I do not ever expect to get a call or email from them because I left my card at the venue. Every now and then it happens and I feel lucky to get that call. Perhaps I have left my card at a venue and the next day, a musician on the roster calls out sick. Maybe then the venue representative will call me to see if I can fill in, and this might be my chance to get on the roster. But like I said, it is rare. The one thing I can do to try to control the outcome is to initiate contact. I can always pat myself on the back for trying. I don't want to be a SAM who complains that I have left my card at a venue five times and never been called. I have no complaints if I have done my best and contacted them. I just keep trying to get a gig. In the audition section of this book, I will tell you how it took *fifteen years* to finally get a response from one place, and I still needed to go do an audition. But I did get gigs on my calendar and will probably continue to play there once a month for years to come. I know for a fact I would not be playing there at all if I had just kept dropping off my card in hopes that someone from the venue would contact me first to book a gig.

It can help if your card is somehow one of a kind. Companies like VistaPrint, which I have ordered my cards from many times, are great and they have lots of templates for us to use. My first business card, when I moved to Florida and changed my phone number, was made with one of these templates. It didn't take long for a manager to show me another SAM's business card using the same template. I was new to town and I was out at various venues, networking with other musicians. I was handed a lot of business cards and if I remember correctly, I ended up with a collection of them all using the same template. The only differences were the fonts, text color, and information. The background picture was the same so they were basically identical, and it would be easy to confuse one from another. None of them stood out at all, and I knew right away that I needed a new business card.

A friend who is a graphic artist helped me put one of my personal pictures on the front of my new business card. Later I added the QR code on the back. I have been using this design for many years now and no other Solo Acoustic Musicians have handed me one that looks like mine. If you can't figure out how to do something like this on your own and you can't get a friend to help you, my suggestion is to use the website Fiverr.com. Someone there can help you make a unique business card, with a personal touch, for very little money.

A unique and well-designed business card is just another professional touch to add to your lifestyle as a SAM.

AGENTS AND BUSINESS CARDS

I currently work with an agent named Jane McKee, who is one of the interviewees in this book. Two months ago, I played my first gig at a venue that she put me into, and the general manager asked me for my card. I gladly gave him my card and told him to please let Jane know if he liked me or if he didn't like me. Now there are a few reasons I did this. The first is that Jane works with a lot of musicians, and I know from previous experiences with other agencies that it can be really easy to get lost in the shuffle. If a venue is really busy and a general manager likes the musician, they might not have time or the chance to make a note on their calendar. They might make a mental note and then maybe two weeks later when they talk to the agent, they might get it mixed up. When a venue is going through an agent for booking, they aren't typically getting to know all of the musicians personally. It can lead to being told that they don't like you when they did, or that they do like a musician when they didn't, etc.

Jane has booked me at the bar part of several chain restaurants, and I've always made it a point after my gig to go to the manager and give them my card. I follow this up by saying to them, "Please call Jane and tell her if you like me or not. I want you to get my name right and it's okay if you don't like me and it's okay if you do like me. I just don't want you to get the names mixed up."

I'm pretty sure that because I gave managers my business card, at locations Jane booked for me, I got booked back at those places. I think every time I've done it the manager has come over to me and said something like, "Wow! We really like you. You did really well tonight. Here's your check."

I reply by saying, "Thank you. I want to make sure that you tell Jane what you just said to me, so here's my business card. I would like to play here again as well, so make sure you tell whoever it is at this location who talks to Jane that this is my name." I can even go on record and say that there's been a handful of times now that I have received an email or phone call from Jane the next day asking me, "What did you do at that venue last night? They loved you."

I just made sure somebody knew who I was. I didn't ask the manager to book a gig behind the agency's back. I'm not going to take a gig from that manager if they call me without going through Jane, because she's the one I have to show appreciation to for the gig. While some other musicians may think they can cut corners and cheat around the back way to get a gig in that way, it's not who I am. If ever a manager from that chain of venues were to call me behind Jane's back, I would know something was wrong and I would talk to them nicely, and then I would call Jane and tell her what just happened because there has to be a certain amount of loyalty between her and me. You have to protect that loyalty, professionalism, ethics, and morals. You have to maintain the relationship you've built with someone who could call me up to offer me a gig. A manager could offer me $1,000 to play for an hour at a private party and I would have to say, well, that's great and all but we have to call Jane. Do you see what I mean? What if the manager called me and said I want you to come to play at a friend's catered hotel party? Whatever it is, it doesn't really matter because it was all generated and originated through my contact with Jane. I would want her to get her percentage, and I would also want to protect my calendar or not lose future gigs with Jane. It is just not worth taking the chance, because the steady money is worth much more to my calendar and my stability as a Solo Acoustic Musician.

A few years ago when I was on a gig that was booked by a different agent, this concept didn't work out so well for me. Now, I don't give up easily and I have been able to repair the bridge that was burned, but I don't get as many gigs as I used to from that agent. I wouldn't normally take more than one or two gigs a month from any agent, because I don't like to put all my eggs in one basket and I'm confident in my ability to book myself. I have known other SAMs who have told me stories of having a falling out with an agent and subsequently losing all the gigs on their calendar. It can become very easy to get lazy by only playing gigs that are booked through an agent. Unfortunately, I was not able to convince this particular agent to do an interview for the book, and I think it's because she knew that I would bring up this specific topic. But this is what happened between her and me from my perspective.

After almost 3 years of working together often and very successfully, we had built what I thought was a good rapport. Most of the gigs that she booked for me were private parties, corporate functions, sports teams, and airports. They usually paid very well. I always wore appropriate wardrobe, showed up on time, and did a good job. On top of that, I always tried to communicate with the client, who might be a representative of a sports team or the owner of a construction company having their 30th anniversary party.

One night when I was playing in a high-class steakhouse inside a casino, a man came into the lounge and was looking around strangely. He walked straight to my merch table and then looked up at me on the stage. He asked, "Do you have a business card?" I was not able to stop in the middle of singing to address him. Then he looked down and said, "Never mind." He picked up a business card from my merchandise table and walked away. Well, needless to say, before the end of the gig that evening, my phone was blowing up — and it's not good business to react emotionally, it should have been a logical rational non-emotional response that this agent had with me but instead, she went full-bore angry slash crazy. My phone was ringing off the hook while texts were repeatedly dinging my notifications. I knew something was wrong. I later found out that the guy who picked up my card was the agent's husband. I even recall the next day telling her how she should have tested her theory by having someone else, like a friend of hers, call me and try to book a gig. I would have asked that person where did they get my card, and they would have had to say that place. I would have told them that is a gig I booked through so-and-so agency and you'll have to call such-and-such person. I would have followed that by giving the person the agency's contact information, and then I would have called the agency to give them the client information. But that's not what happened, and so the phone calls and emails went on for a couple of weeks and she canceled me eight months' worth of gigs that I already had booked with her. But I never took more than two or three gigs a month from her, and that was a really smart move on my part because things fell apart fast and furious.

I was never relying on that individual or her company to fill my calendar. She has at least ten employees and I probably could have had even more gigs through them, but I never took more than I thought I should. Once again, I'm not telling any of you how to do what you do; I'm telling you what I did and hoping that you can learn from my experience. Part of what sucked for me was trying to explain to her that I had been doing this for more than a year and a half and that I had already told her that I was doing it. I was putting my card right next to hers on my merch table, beside my tip can and CDs for sale. The reason I did this is that one of the employees at the agency called me one day and said a new potential client had called, because they saw a guy playing at the airport but didn't know who it was. She asked me if I was the musician that the client was talking about. I asked about the date on the calendar, but her response was that she didn't know. I told her that I had no idea what day it was or who the person was. Evidently, the new potential client didn't know either.

(Sidebar: we can all look up what day we took a plane flight. We could also look up all the days that I was playing at the airport. But this was sometime around two months later and I had no idea what day or what person this could be. I played music in that airport 10 times a month for several months in a row for the agency. I would think it wouldn't have been hard for the potential client to look up the day and time of their flight.)

This was the point in my conversation with the agent where I explained to her that it probably wasn't me, because I give everybody my card and her card at the same time. They were not happy that I was doing that. They told me, "You're not allowed to do that. It's our biggest rule of things not to do." I explained that this was exactly the type of situation I was trying to avoid, because here you have a potential client calling you to hire somebody but they don't know who it was they saw playing. I want them to know who I am, because if they like me, I want them to tell you they like me, and if they don't like me, I want them to tell you that. But I want them to get my name right either way.

I proposed to the agency that we make me a card with their name, phone number, email address, and website, but also my name as the musician. It could say Michael Nichols - Solo Acoustic Musician and then list all the agency's information. That way, there would be no way for the potential client to call me. Yes, somebody probably could find me online by name without much hassle at all. That doesn't happen very often, though, and if someone did find me through an internet search and contact me, I would ask them where they had seen me play and tell them, "You have to talk to the agency about booking me, because that gig was booked by her and I have a contract with them."

Shortly before all this happened, I played a private party for the 30th anniversary of a construction company. It was a good time, though there were a few issues that were sorted out pretty easily. I think I talked about one issue in SAM 1 where the owner, Mike, dropped my mic onto the ground and basically destroyed it. They gave me the money to replace it, so that was fine, but more importantly, the owner's wife asked for my card, explaining that she wanted it for the explicit purpose of hiring me without going through the agency. I gave her my card and the agency card and said, "I can't do that because I have signed a contract with them that prohibits me from doing something like that. But I would love to play any kind of event for you, your family, or your business. Again, you guys were great, and thank you for hiring me." After that, I left and headed home.

As I was driving, I thought about the situation. I don't know how long the agency had known this client, or anything about the level of communication they have with each other. The situation just seemed off to me, and I thought that maybe it was a test by the agency. No other clients they had sent me to had ever asked me to book a gig without them. It felt like I was being set up, and I felt good about following the rules and doing the right thing.

Music is spiritual. The music business is not.
—Claudio Monteverdi

About a year and a half later, I got an email asking me if I would like to play a private party and it turned out to be a member of the family that owns the construction company. At first, I thought, screw it; the other people fired me over this whole business card fiasco. But then I thought it might be an interesting way to mend a burned bridge. So I called the agency that had booked me for the original anniversary party and explained the new situation. I had tried to make up with them before, but I thought this potential gig would be a great way to finally get it done. I told them that the previous client had emailed me via my business card and asked me to play a party. I asked them to contact the client on my behalf, and requested $400 to do the party, and that the agency could charge whatever their usual fees were on top of that. I was proving to them that I was loyal. The fact that they had gotten me gigs meant something to me, and I wasn't trying to screw them over. Doing this went a long way to rebuilding the burnt bridge, and that agency has offered me some new gigs.

Honestly, part of me thought enough time had passed that I could have just booked that gig on my own. But again, it could have been a test to get me in trouble. I was in a contract with a five-year clause forbidding me from working with clients that had previously been booked through the agency. Still, it wasn't fear so much as it was logic, after I sat on the beach in my chair thinking for a little bit. I thought this gave me leverage, to prove what I said was true and that I would do the right thing. I thought it could be a way to mend the relationship with that agency, so it was worth the phone call. I try to stay truthful and do what I think is right, ethical, and moral. I never had any intention of going behind anybody's back or cheating the agency out of their fees.

I've said all that to say this: If you ever work with an agency, ask them immediately about making a business card with your name on it. I've got an even better idea: agencies should provide business cards with all their information and a line where the musician can write their own name on it. They should give these out so that all the musicians that they are sending out to gigs can put them on their merch/tip table. If this can't be arranged, offer to pay for and print up a batch of cards with the agency's information, and your name.

The most important thing is if you work with an agent, you need to have some way to let venues know your name and also who represents you. Honestly, I'm frustrated writing this right now because this agency should have figured this out on their own years ago. I didn't have any ulterior motive in putting my card beside theirs; I just wanted to get credit for what I was doing, and if someone wanted to book me, I wanted them to know who I was. I tried to explain this in a rather long email that was received very poorly. I tried to explain in phone calls. I tried to explain with an impromptu in-person visit to their office. But they were very angry and it did not help me at all to remind them of our conversation from a year and a half earlier, when I explained what I was doing and why. I wish I had come up with my combo business card idea earlier because everyone involved could have avoided all this confusion and anger.

At the end of the day, we have to try to do our best and remember to try to be professional and not lose our cool. Always stay calm and be nice. And never put too many eggs in one basket, because things can sometimes go sour real quick. I hope this struggle that I went through can help you avoid a similar situation in the future, and may help you make good decisions when it comes to dealing with business cards and talent agents.

 **PROMO VIDEO**

In SAM 1, I barely touched on the subject of promo videos. I know many musicians, and most of them have a promo video. Each of them has done theirs a little differently. First I'll tell you what I did, and then I'll talk about some other ideas or options that you could also try.

The first thing I did was create a post on social media asking if anyone knew of someone who could help make a video for me. I got more than twenty responses and contacted one of them online and by phone. The conversation was great and our ideas meshed very well. I thought it would be good to shoot at a place I play that is not open for lunch, only for dinner. It had a front and back porch, a front and back dining room, and two different lounges in between. I did a little coordinating between the cameraman/videographer and the general manager of the venue to set up a date and time. They open the doors at 5 PM, and I think we were there from 1 PM to 2:30 PM.

What I did was set up my normal gig gear in one dining room and on the back porch as well. I only played parts of the songs: a verse and chorus of one, a chorus of another, and a guitar solo from a third that involved building a loop to play over. I tried to showcase different styles of music and skill sets. I played parts of a rock song, an upbeat reggae song, and a country ballad. Then I moved to a different part of the venue, to make it seem like I was in different places. I also played in two spots without my P.A., microphone, or pedals, using only my guitar and voice.

Each time I moved, I appeared to change location, because each room of this venue is completely different. They have various murals on the walls. The back porch has a whole different environment from the front porch. I also changed my shirt and added a hat for certain shots. The end result comes off as if I was at four different places at different times.

Even if you shoot a video at home, you can play a few parts of songs in your living room with the mantle and fireplace behind you, and then go to the backyard and shoot some outdoor footage. As I did, changing your clothes — from a blue shirt to a green or an orange one and maybe a ball cap, then maybe no hat or a tropical beach hat or something — can add variety. You are still in the same location, but you're making use of the things that are available to you. It makes your video a little more exciting than just having the same blank wall or the same fireplace in the background for the whole thing.

Speaking of time, many people have said promo videos should be two to three minutes long. But as I sometimes take things over the top, my video is five minutes long. I was very fortunate to have shot two segments of my video without any microphone or amplifier, because I didn't have to move and set up again. It was just me and my guitar, but in the other two sections, I had to tear down and set up my gig gear again.

I was very trusting and let the person that shot the video edit it as well, and he did a great job. In the past, I just shot footage with my phone and a friend edited it for free. This time I spent $300 to hire this guy and he did a great job. I had never met him before, but we became friends, and I would like to shoot a new promo video with him sometime because I've learned so many new songs.

He showed up on time because I had told him that it was very important to me. He also had a very professional camera and an expensive external microphone to really pick up the audio. After we shot the video, a couple of weeks went by as he worked on the editing. I surprised myself because I didn't want any changes. I thought it was very creative and he did a really good job. One cool thing about having the external microphone was that he could layer my music over video without it having the same sound. So when he was shooting video he was being creative and doing things like shooting my feet while I was stepping on pedals and my hands while I was playing the guitar. None of it had to match per se, but at the same time he did use authentic audio and video so that my voice and everything lined up with the songs.

I think I chose ten different songs, and I did basically thirty-second segments which added up to five minutes total. Many venue representatives have told me that it is creative and it looks like I put a lot of effort into my video. Every now and then I call the guy and say, "Dude, I just booked gigs at several more new venues that pay really good money because of my professional video."

It's okay if you can't afford to pay someone to make a video, but if you shoot it yourself think about some of the ideas I've suggested. Even if it's just going from your living room to your backyard or the park down the street or something like that. If you can get someone to shoot the video, they can even walk around you in a circle so that there are different views. They can shoot footage from an angle on the side or behind you or from your feet up to your head or just your hands on the guitar. It is to your advantage to try to be creative with this process in hopes that your video will stand out and be noticed.

I know some people that have set up video shoots at gigs. They invite all of their friends to dance and jump around in front of them to show that they are a party band that has fun with the crowd. In my case, as a Solo Acoustic Musician, I don't think it really helps me to do that. I don't want the venue to expect me to bring a bunch of people, and I'm not usually playing to a bunch of people who are screaming, dancing or jumping around. Most of my venues don't have a big stage or a dance floor. I chose to shoot video of myself in a quiet environment where I can give an accurate depiction of my skill sets. I want the venue representative to be able to clearly hear me play guitar and sing.

Thinking about location can be crucial, and I've been thinking about where I might shoot a new video. I live in a condo complex that includes a pool building with an extra room for hosting parties, complete with a kitchen, a big screen, and even a pool table. The H.O.A. office, gym, and racquetball court are also in this building. Nobody uses the racquetball court, though, and I could likely convince the nice lady in the office to let me play music in there for an hour and a half. I believe it might stand out if a venue representative clicks on the link.

Setting up in a specifically chosen location, shooting footage, and editing it is different than having your girlfriend hold their phone up while you're performing in a bar somewhere, with random background people potentially cursing or yelling things during the songs you wanted to include in your video. It's also important to realize that even if no one is inappropriate, you are still going to have that crowd noise in the mix. Cell phones were designed to pick up human voices. You may be playing forty feet away from any people, and there may only be twenty of them at the bar. The phone will prioritize all of their voices over your guitar. It will sound like you're in a really loud room, even though it's kind of empty, and it will overtake the phone's ability to record clear audio of your music. The phone might also cut your bass frequencies, and that might not showcase what you actually sound like.

The fact that I spent money on my video is relevant because it has landed me so many new residual clients that it really is a successful investment. You already know how we have to buy speakers, cables, strings, business cards, and build websites. A proper, professionally made video was something I decided was worth the investment because it is my sales pitch. It's going to help me get gigs, which are going to put the money in my bank account and pay my bills.

As I became friends with Dave, I actually got to learn more about him. He shoots photos and video for touring national acts and big concerts. It was a really cool experience working with him. The next time I make a promo video, whether it's with him or someone else, I also have this experience to draw from and it will be just as good if not better. I will be proud of the product and I will be happy to send out my links in emails. I know I will book a lot of gigs with my video. It was $300 well spent, and if you have the opportunity or the ability and the budget, you should pull the trigger on doing something similar.

Here are some things that my friends have told me in the past about promo videos. I remember many conversations with Solo Acoustic Musicians on this subject.

Keep the video between two to three minutes. Play a fast song, a slow song, a blues, a country song, and a rock song. Show different styles and genres. Play songs from the 70s, 80s, 90s, and 2000s. My video features thirty-second segments, but you could include just a few lines out of a verse or a chorus and put together a compilation of ten song parts in two minutes. I will say as an artist it really is up to you to decide how you want to assemble your video, musically speaking. But when it comes to the behind-the-scenes and technical matters, I think it's good to get a little advice and then put your own spin on it.

Since I wrote SAM 1, I have made a lot of new friends from all around the world and all around the country. It's been interesting to see promo videos that they have made. I've seen a lot of them that were shot at one gig, and I thought maybe they should get footage from three or four different venues. One of the videos I saw even showed the musician talking to people at their table, maybe before he played or when he was on a break. The fact that they interact with the audience members might be of interest to a venue representative. One of them had the camera zoom-in on their tip can. There are quite a few different variations of videos that I've seen.

It might be cool to do something based on where you live. I think it would stand out if I went on a boat ride with a friend, or a rented catamaran sunset cruise with a bunch of strangers, and brought my guitar. If I asked everybody to be quiet for three to five minutes, I could sing parts of a few songs to add to my video. I live by the beach in Florida and being out on a boat in my video would be geographically appropriate. It would stand out as something different when a venue representative saw it.

One of the previous promo videos I made was in a local brewery, with big stacks of barrels behind me. If you live near a brewery or winery, I'm sure the owner or manager would give you permission to shoot a few minutes of video. You can even add more locations to it later. I have gone to local parks, and outside of a library where there was a fountain and green trees, and these were cool locations to do a video shoot.

The nature of the music business is such that it's better to have a few chances for some things to be successful than just one, and that's kind of been my attitude all along.
—Adam Schlesinger

I'm pretty sure that you could find some interesting places like lunchtime at a bowling alley and you would probably be allowed to stand in a lane if you rented the shoes. Another thought I had once was to take an elevator to the top floor of a 20-floor hotel and find a window overlooking the city and shoot some video. It would be fun to get footage in the elevator as well. One song on the way up and one on the way down. Don't be afraid to experiment and come up with creative ideas for places with interesting backgrounds.

Now here's another trick: whether you're making a video yourself or hiring someone to make it for you, make two versions. (They should not be charging you for two versions; just make sure you bring this up in the beginning and don't add it on at the end of the project.)

Your initial video will go out via email and text messages to venue representatives for the sole purpose of booking gigs, and you will want to put your name, phone number, email, and/or website at the beginning and sometimes even at the end of the video, perhaps accompanied by "available for booking" or something about yourself like "blues music" or "folk acoustic artist" or even "Solo Acoustic Musician."

But you also need a version of your promo video with no contact information, because agents will want one they can show to their clients. If it has your contact information, their clients could bypass them and their fees by calling you directly, as in the story discussed earlier. So remember to make a version of your promo video specifically for agents. You can add that information to the sales pitch paragraph that you send agents in emails. Let them know that you have multiple videos, and that you sent them the one that is agent-appropriate. There has to be a give and take when you're working with someone else, and you have to let them know that you will protect that relationship.

I hope you all have fun making a really cool promo video, but I also hope that you make three, four, or five of them over the next year and really step it up each time. It's important to learn to do things better and get more professional at whatever it is that we are doing.

I'm sure you will make awesome promo videos and get lots of gigs.

High five!

 **AUDITION**

Last week, I was drinking a cup of coffee and learning some songs at my high-top desk when my phone rang. It was around 11 AM on a Monday morning, and the Entertainment Manager of my steady Monday-evening gig was calling to tell me that they were having electrical problems in the tiki bar and would have to cancel the music for that evening. I later found out they had to cancel music three days in a row before they could get the problem fixed.

I wasn't too bummed out, because I have been busy working hard and playing a lot. I thought I could use the night off. I decided to break my Monday routine and go to the beach and read a book. While I was there, I thought about still making it a work day and getting something done. I would go "gig fishing." This is a term I use when I get into my car, go for a drive, and stop into places to try to get a gig. I drop off my card, which is the bait, and I gather information while "trolling my boat" or slowly driving my van looking for the next spot to stop.

I have lived in the same area for almost fifteen years now and I am pretty familiar with what's going on in the music scene. But things are always changing, and spots come and go. Although I am up to date with my online search and email activities for booking gigs, it is always a good practice to get out there in person and do some networking. Putting in the work is another way to think of it. I didn't wake up that morning thinking I'd be driving around and looking for gigs but there I was, headed north to another town nine miles away, and stopping on the way up and back down at any place that I know has music or is a new place that might have music. I keep business cards in my car's console and I am always ready to give my sales pitch.

In business, you can have one massive success that earns $50 million overnight, and that's it. You're successful. End of story. But in the music business, you have to keep on doing it.
—Noel Gallagher

I stopped in at five places that evening. The one place I am going to tell you about has a backstory. The first year I moved to the area, I approached the place on a gig fishing trip much like this one. I have never spoken to the owners once, though I have been there at least a dozen times and left my card with an employee every single time. I have repeatedly called, emailed, social media messaged, and even texted the owner's cell phone because it was listed on their business card.

At this point, I am fourteen years into living here and I have never talked to any venue representative about playing at this venue. I know other people who have played here, and I know people who have just moved to the Tampa area and have managed to get on the calendar. I am being honest that it is like a dead zone to me because they have never called me back or emailed me back, and every time I have stopped in, I have been told the owner is not there right now. I honestly have never understood how anybody got a gig booked at this place, and yet the calendar has stayed full three to five days a week.

So, I stopped in again. I had heard that there were some changes being made in management. The place was a pizza/wings/burgers restaurant/sports bar, etc., a family-friendly neighborhood place with large indoor and outdoor seating areas with a bar located in each. They also have a stage designated for live music, so people go there to hear Solo Acoustic Musicians and bands.

Once again, I dropped off my card with the bartender, and I also went inside to the hostess stand and gave her one. The bartender told me the hostess had a business card for the manager in charge of booking the music. I noted that she did not say the owner. But the hostess didn't have any cards for the manager, and wouldn't give me a name or any contact information. The only thing she would do was pass on my card. That was when she slipped and said, "I will give it to the manager when she is here tomorrow night."

When I got home, I went to their website and tried emailing them, but the address came back undeliverable, so I decided to let them know something was wrong with their email or website.

When I called the next evening, the hostess answered the phone. I told her who I was and asked to speak to the manager. She told me the manager was busy and I said, "I will hold to speak with her. I have been trying for quite some time to speak to the manager about the music calendar and I would only need a moment to chat."

My persistence paid off and the manager came to the phone. We talked for more than five minutes, which was longer than I expected. I was able to gather information about changes being made to the musicians' roster and get personal contact information for the manager in charge of booking the calendar. After almost fifteen years, I had finally spoken with someone, and the conversation went well. After the phone call, I sent her my email pitch with the YouTube link for my promo video. During our conversation, I offered to "audition" for one hour for free on an off-day afternoon or evening. The next day I was invited to come in the next week on Tuesday evening from 6 to 7 PM. We texted back and forth a little bit and confirmed the details.

A week went by and every time I saw the audition on my calendar, I would think about what songs to play to impress them during a one-hour set. I was confident that I would do well, but I still had some nerves building up, because I hadn't done a "labeled audition" in quite a while. I have played new places recently and, in a way, a paid first gig in a new venue is an audition. This was different, though, because I was being given a $30 food and drink tab to play. This was not a paying gig — it was for the sole purpose of getting a paid gig.

I arrived right at 5 PM to load in and set up. I parked my cart by the stage and went to the bar to introduce myself to as many employees as possible. I asked for the manager as well, but she wasn't there. The bartender said that it was the manager's night off, but that she would probably come in for the audition. Two bad things: the manager wasn't there, and it was her night off. One good thing: the bartender knew I was coming in and auditioning.

I texted the manager that I was there and that I had checked in with the bartender. Then I tried not to stress out or think that the manager wasn't coming to see me or had forgotten about my audition. I got set up, and then I had time to relax. I chatted with a couple of regular customers for a few minutes and checked my phone. I still had not received a response from the manager, so at 5:30 PM I called her directly and she answered. I was happy to hear that she would be there in about fifteen minutes.

I was itching to play so I asked the bartender to cut the music and started playing music at 5:45 PM. While I had been setting up and hanging out the number of customers in the restaurant had tripled, so I was thankful to have an audience to play for. Right before I started, I had coordinated my volume level with the bartender but I still made sure, after the first and second songs, to ask her if I was too loud or too soft. She said my volume was just right. The truth was, I turned up a little bit twice and was feeling out the room with my volume knob.

I like to engage the audience and interact with people by asking them questions about what kind of songs they like or what they feel like hearing. I will pick out a table and ask them if they would like to hear a rock, reggae, blues, or country song. After playing that song I will pick another table and ask them if they would like to hear a song from the '70s, '80s, '90s, or 2000s and beyond. Sometimes a table will pick rock and then I will add the decade's question for a double choice. Example − '80s rock.

The manager arrived during my first song and was definitely paying attention to what I was doing. She was evaluating my musical abilities, but I could tell she was enjoying the way I was engaging the customers and getting them involved in the show. I told a couple of stories along the way and smiled a lot because I was having fun. I made $47.00 in tips during my one-hour and fifteen-minute set. I mixed in a couple of looper songs I play and showcased different genres from different eras. I was conscientiously watching the room for people leaning in to talk and didn't see any of that going on, so I didn't think I was playing too loud. I did gradually play a little more aggressively, but I kept in mind I was playing during the middle of a Tuesday evening dinner service.

One thing that stood out when I was talking to the manager afterward was that she said musicians didn't want to audition, and she was thankful that I took the time to come down and play a set. In more than one way I have gone above and beyond to get a gig in this venue. She didn't need to hear me ramble on about all the years I had been trying to talk to someone and book a date. It felt good for her to express gratitude for me coming down to audition. I am always hungry for work and eager for new clients, and although I have years of experience, I keep myself humble enough to realize that I still need to audition sometimes. After all, I probably wouldn't be getting a gig here at all if I didn't.

She confided in me that she was new to booking musical acts and that during the last six months, she had hired and paid some musicians who were really bad and unprofessional. She told me about attitude problems, playing too loud, drinking too much, etc. On top of all that, she was receiving complaints from her regular clientele, who were unhappy with some of these acts' musical abilities as well. I assured her that I do not drink on the gig, I show up on time, I communicate well if there is a problem or need for a cancellation, and that I am overall a professional on the job.

The end result was that I booked some dates on the calendar. I only live a few miles away and I had some Thursday evenings open, so this worked out great for me. She books three months out and I booked dates in January, February, and March of 2023. I know I will do well in this venue and it will be a steady residual client, booking once a month at the minimum. She even asked me if I was available for a regular Tuesday or Wednesday shift and hinted that she is trying to convince the owners to let her hire a Solo Acoustic Musician for one or both of those days. She thought I would be a perfect fit.

The manager received many compliments about me from customers while I was on the stage. I made enough tips during a short amount of time to let me know that I was very well received by the audience. Overall, this audition was a success. I have landed a new client and will probably play here for a long time.

You might not want to do an audition, and I can't really do this kind of thing every time I want to book a gig, but it has its place in the process of keeping a calendar full. Try to remember that you can always offer to do one if you think it can help you get your foot in the door of a venue. Just put your best foot forward (pun intended) and give it a try.

 **QUERY LETTER**

A query letter is a one-page proposal that you send to an agent, editor, or publishing house. In a query letter, a writer will pitch their work or idea to generate interest from agents or editors. The work could be a novel, magazine article, or nonfiction book.

A query letter is the first step in the process for an author to sell their manuscript or written material.

For a Solo Acoustic Musician, a query letter is a one-page written introduction that you send to a venue representative or an agent to introduce yourself and start a dialogue about booking a gig.

I think you should have at least three different basic query letters. They will be similar but will have differences based on the context of the venue or gig situation. Always remember to tailor your letter to a specific potential client. For example, you might want to add something to your letter if it is a sales pitch for a private party. Maybe a sentence about being able to provide a microphone to accommodate a special announcement or speech if one of the hosts would like to speak.

It's called the music business. We've all gone into it 'cause we love the music, and a lot of people end up with nothing at the end of the day, after they've done all of this great music, 'cause they never learned any of the business side.
—Vinnie Paul

A short paragraph about who you are and what you do should suffice. You may want to send a casual, short, direct letter to a local restaurant or bar, but add a little more information for a bigger venue or corporate client. At this point, you have to develop your own personal tastes when it comes to this part of the process.

Some SAMs will add a list of other venues they have previously played, a list of the songs they are currently playing, and a description of their previous experience. I like to have a focused pitch to interest them in watching my promo video. Remember, these are busy people that we are selling to, and they are bombarded with other musicians' sales pitches. You want to be brief and get their attention without dragging on and on. Get them to your video as quickly as you can and hope they like what you have presented to them.

If you have a website or a promo video, make sure that it is featured in your letter. Providing that link will make it easier to get someone to watch some of it and hopefully respond. The video is a better sales pitch than any words I could type so I try to be direct and not write too much.

Here is a sample of one of my Solo Acoustic Musician email query letters from the past...

Hello Mr. Smith,

I am interested in joining your entertainment roster.

My name is Michael Nichols and I am available as a solo acoustic musician. I am a full-time working musician and this is how I make my living. I play a variety of styles including rock, reggae, blues, and country cover songs by a long list of artists.

Here is a link to my promo video.

https://www.youtube.com/watch?v=GRhC-CFJHKUg+==not-a-reallink-to-myvideo-LOL

Michael Nichols

123-456-7890

mymusicwebsite.com

soloacousticmusician.com

I hope you realize that this is not my real phone number, link, or website. LOL

But please do check out soloacousticmusician.com; it is a real website.

REFINING YOUR SALES PITCH

The more familiar you are with all of the information in the checklist/question and answer section, the better you will be able to just hash things out quickly in a conversation. It takes practice and experience. Before pitching any venue representative in person, I suggest making many phone calls with your checklist and answers to their questions right in front of you. Make notes about each conversation. You want to get to know each individual to whom you are selling your service, and how each venue handles their live music booking.

It's important to know the ins and outs of the music business, but you can also dive too deeply into it and forget that you're really here to make music.
—M. Shadows

Make sure you make a note of the date and time that you have contacted someone. You do not want to call them every day. Over-saturating a person with calls and emails can alienate them. Let things breathe. Being patient is a part of sales, and most times it's good to follow up no sooner than a week or two later.

As you refine your pitch, you will get better at selling yourself and your services to complete strangers. Your confidence will build and you will become better at answering their questions. As you grow through practice you should see a higher percentage of your sales pitches turning into booked gigs. It will be a great boost of confidence when you book a gig on the first meeting, phone call, or email. It does happen and it feels awesome! At other times, it may take many attempts to reach someone. Always remember that these are busy people running a business and sometimes the musicians are a luxury and the last thing that they have to deal with.

 # NEGOTIATING A FEE

How do you determine what to charge for a gig?

It can be a simple or complex answer. Some SAMs charge an hourly rate and some break it down by adding together multiple components. They may start with a base rate, with add-ons like mileage or distance, the day of the week, or the size and assumed budget of the venue.

An hourly rate for example could be $50 an hour. So if the gig is three hours (i.e. 6-9 PM) the SAM would ask for $150. The same math would hold true for a four-hour gig (i.e. 6-10 PM) and the answer would be $200. A highly paid SAM might make $100 an hour. It's a goal to build towards this rate.

What is a base rate?

The base rate is the fee you charge for the gig no matter what. If the gig is one hour, then you charge the base rate. It is the starting point of the fee negotiation, and you can add more for extra factors. If the distance to the venue is great, then you can add to your fee. If the length of the gig is more than you typically want to play, then you can add to the fee. If the venue or event coordinator has extra requests, then you can add to the fee. Maybe they want you to learn certain songs or dress a certain way. Maybe they want you to set up early at 3 PM but then you don't start to play until 6 PM; then you can add to your fee. This scenario is possible for a corporate event, a wedding gig, or a private party.

*I may quit the music business
someday, but never the music.*
—Dan Fogelberg

I have been known to add $25 to my fee if the venue doesn't have food or will not provide me with a meal.

An example of a base rate is $200.

Examples of add-ons include:

- $25 meal fee

- $50 distance/mileage fee

- $50-100 for added time (i.e. 6-9 PM for $200 / 6-9:30 PM for $250)

- $100 early setup fee

Sometimes on a gig, the venue or event organizer may ask you to play another 30-60 minutes and of course, you can charge more and add to your fee. The person may approach you on a break or even between songs near the end of your gig. You have to be able to adapt and adjust your set list to add more songs. You also have to be quick with your answer and be firm in your price. As I always say, it's good to be prepared for the situation. You don't want to be slow and uncertain about how to respond. Knowing that you will ask for $100 to stay and play longer will make you decisive and professional. You can phrase it like, "I always charge $100 for an additional __ minutes" or "My fee for additional time is always..." Communicating this should be firm and professional.

# NEGOTIATING A RAISE

Once you have landed a gig, negotiated a fee, and then played at the venue for a while, it can become time to negotiate a raise. Not every place will say yes, but every place is effectively saying no if you don't ask.

It can be hard to get a raise at any job in this world we live in. It's hard to get a raise in a restaurant or bar. Asking for more money is a skill that some people are better at and others need to work on. I think it has to be done with a subtle approach, because they might just cut you from the list if you are too aggressive. People will throw around terms like inflation, cost of living, and gas prices. I personally think it's best to avoid those kinds of reasons for asking for a raise, because everybody has those problems. You don't want to start negotiating a raise in pay by saying, my landlord just raised my rent by $300 a month, so I need more money.

I think the best thing to do is justify why you should get paid $25 or $50 more per gig. In the personal update section of this book, I talk about how many songs I have learned in the past year. I recently received a phone call from a venue manager asking me if I could move from Monday to Saturday night because of the positive responses of customers and staff. According to her, she was getting really good feedback about me and thought that I should be playing on the weekends. I told her as nicely as possible that I was not interested in switching shifts and that I was booked out many months in advance on Saturdays. Also, I didn't want to lose my Monday spot. At the same time, I saw this as an opportunity and some kind of leverage for me to talk to her about more money. This particular gig requires a pretty long drive, and I do it every Monday. I spend a little more than an hour in my van each way. It pays well and I make really good tips, and all of the employees treat me really well. I have a lot of fun interactions with the customers and overall I think it's worth it. I explained to her that I could tell that they really liked me being there and that I have been there for almost a year.

In a polite way, I said to her, "I demonstrated high value with my guitar skills and singing abilities. Beyond that, I have actually upgraded myself throughout the year by adding more songs to my songbook." I pointed out that I was always on time and didn't drink on gigs. (One of the bartenders had told me about a couple of other musicians who played there who got drunk at the gigs.) I also mentioned that I had only had to call out twice — I'm reliable. I reminded her that they had canceled me twice for totally understandable reasons. One was because a hurricane was coming and the other was because there was an electrical problem. I conveyed to her that I appreciated them giving me a couple of days' notice to let me know something was going on at the venue.

The desire to hit a big home run is
dominating the music business.
—Billy Corgan

So I had proved my worth by demonstrating a high value of skills, by being dependable, arriving on time, and communicating well if there was a problem.

I told her I was up to 279 songs, which is a lot of new music. The employees and some of the regulars tell me that they enjoy the fact that I don't play the same songs every week, and that clearly I have learned a lot of new songs. They really enjoy the fact that I mix it up and that my show is different every time. I have asked every single employee what kind of music they like and what specific bands they like. I have learned some Johnny Cash songs for one bartender and some Tyler Childers songs for another. I learned a Led Zeppelin song for a barback. One bartender really likes old reggae, and another bartender really likes classic rock. The employees have been taking turns telling me that I'm one of their favorites and that they want me there twice a week, though I don't think that works out logistically with my drive time, the gas and mileage, and the wear and tear on my vehicle.

Hearing these things also gave me a feeling of confidence and leverage for asking for some more money. The employees don't make the decision whether I get a raise or not, but it made me feel good when it seemed like every week one of them asked, "Can we get you here another day of the week?" That let me know that they were probably saying that to the boss as well. I told them all that I would love to come down another night, but I didn't think it was logistically probable unless I moved half an hour closer.

I didn't want to lose my Monday gig and I didn't want to switch to a different night, because Monday is the hardest night to find a steady gig. I really liked the arrangement as it was. All of this made negotiating a raise a lot easier. I had every confidence that things would go my way, as long as I wasn't forceful, greedy, demanding, or needy.

When negotiating a raise, just go in and talk about what you have done to improve yourself. In my mind, this is the same at almost any job. There are differences, of course, because I'm personally dealing with maybe a hundred different venue representatives at any given time. Somebody else might be at the same job with the same boss for five years; that is a different dynamic, but I think some of the principles still hold true.

Let's say you are a cook or chef and you went and took some new cooking lessons. Or if you are an electrician and you take classes to upgrade your certifications and skill level, you should be able to go into the office and talk to the manager or the owner and ask nicely for a raise. You don't want to make a demand.

I will add that I probably come off a little weak sometimes because I begin by telling them this is not an ultimatum. I don't want to rock the boat and I don't want to be fired. I want a pat on the back for doing a good job. I don't need a 100% pay raise. $25 a gig. $50 a gig. If the gig is paying $200 or $225 and they raised me to $250, then that's great. It doesn't have to be a $100 or $200 dollar raise. In the same way, you wouldn't walk into a corporate office or a skilled labor job and ask for a 50% bump in your yearly salary or hourly rate, because that would probably come off as way too aggressive.

But I have also learned that I think I wait too long to ask for a raise. So I've decided I need to be a little more aggressive with my timing. Going forward, every year or two, I'm going to talk to people about a little bump up in pay. I know how long I've been playing at every venue. I know what I get paid at each venue and it's all different. I know what I'm paid by a big corporate hotel and I know what I'm paid by a small local brewery. I know that all of them have different budgets. Also, I pay attention over time to how much rapport I build with the venue representative that I would need to talk to about a raise. Communicating with each one of them is a different scenario. I'm making notes in my calendar charts or in my log book because I've gone 5, 6, 8, or 10 years at certain spots and never asked for a raise when I probably should have. I am making notes to plan ahead to ask each venue for a raise.

I have had places give me a raise without me asking for one, which is awesome. At the end of the gig, a manager hands me the check and says, "Hey, we like what you're doing, so we took you from $175 to $200." I remember a place that took me from $150 to $175 to $200 to $225 a gig over a few years. I never even asked for a raise one time. I think that's awful nice, because that shows that they actually paid attention to what I was doing and they noticed I'd made improvements or developed better skills. They could see that I was demonstrating value for the venue. It is nice to feel appreciated.

There are a couple of restaurants where I play that aren't much fun for me, because I just sit in the corner and play songs. I'm kind of quiet in between songs because that's the vibe of that gig. Then there are other places where I talk to the audience in between songs because it's a little livelier; the atmosphere makes it acceptable for me to engage the audience in that way. I understand every venue can be different. Sometimes a manager or bartender tells me, "Man you really got the audience interested tonight, and that's awesome, because they were all having a lot of fun." They will tell me about other musicians who just sit there with a withdrawn look and body language and don't smile. Six months or a year later, you can add a thing like that to your list of reasons you should get a raise.

Some people add dance moves. Some people tell jokes. I choose to talk to the audience more and find out what they like. Another potential strategy is if you can show that you have improved your average tips per gig. I don't want to actually show them a calendar or my personal spreadsheet, but I can back such an assertion up if I have to, with the actual information. I just want to be able to explain to a venue representative that my tips went from $31 on average per gig two years ago to $67 in tips per gig on average this year. By tracking my numbers and keeping up with my logbook and spreadsheets, I now know for certain that I have improved. I am doing something better, and I know this for sure because the proof is showing up in my tip can. If I wasn't performing better at playing guitar, singing, working the crowd, and entertaining them then I would see no difference in my tips. But clearly, there is a change and it's a good one.

I could even be venue specific about my tips when I am negotiating, like with the Monday gig I was talking about. I could go over my calendar for the previous year and total up what I made in tips every Monday to tell the venue representative, "Wow! Look at all these tips I made; clearly people in your venue like me." With my overall calendar more than doubling my tip per gig average, I can see a statistical indicator that something has changed for the better. I can say to the venue representative, the people in the audience are paying me a little more because I'm doing a good job, so I'm asking you for a little bit more pay as well.

Sometimes it will be hard to do, and there may be a little bit of fear or hesitancy to go to a venue representative and state your case for a raise. Part of this is timing. When is the right time to ask for a raise? You might not want to make your move right after the general manager was fired. The owner might be busy trying to find a new manager, and frustrated with other things going on, and it might not be a good time to get on their radar by asking for more money. It helps you to pay attention and know a little bit about the dynamics in the venue if you can.

Sometimes it's a good idea to just plant a seed and talk to the venue representative about the future. Putting parameters on the timeline for getting a raise can be a good way to start. "A few months from now or starting in the new year, I would like to talk to you about bumping up my pay." Tell them about how you have improved your gig performance and give them your pitch or list of things you've been doing to improve. You can even mention in conversation, "I've been doing these things to improve my skills, and these other things to improve my shows. I'm doing all this because I want to get a raise. I am going to continue to keep getting better at all of these parts of my job. I really enjoy being part of your team and on the entertainment roster in your venue." Throw in some stuff like, "I really appreciate you guys working with me and being understanding when I had to call out sick. So I just wanted to let you know what I've been up to so we can come back and talk about it in a couple of months. I want you to know that it is something I want to do in the near future." Don't make it seem like an ultimatum or a demand, or be aggressive. It also gives them time to think about what they would be willing to negotiate, to look at their books and think about what you said.

If you just walk into the office and say, "I need $100 more per gig starting right now or I'm not playing here anymore," then you've probably just talked yourself right out of a gig. I'm always prepared for someone to tell me no, and that's okay. Last year when I was talking to almost all of my venues about a raise, I did it very nicely. The manager of a place I played every Wednesday agreed to give me a $50 raise, and then two weeks later the owner fired me. She was never there, but she came in at the end of my gig, while I was packing up, and handed me cash. She told me, "We no longer need you." Then she walked back into the kitchen and disappeared. I could handle that. It wasn't very nice of her to do it that way, but oh well.

I would have stayed on for my previous pay, but somehow that was not an option, or even something I could discuss with that owner. It was unfortunate, and it didn't help that she was not the person with whom I had negotiated and discussed the raise. Another venue representative who said no to my request came back to me and spoke very politely. He explained that he just didn't have the money to give me another fifty bucks every time I was there, and I was okay with that. It was a good conversation and only strengthened our relationship. I still play there once a month. That's what I mean by not presenting a request as an ultimatum. I still want to play these places. I just want a little financial pat on the back for doing a good job.

# CONTRACTS

There is a conversation I've had many times with other musicians, and of course friends and family. It usually starts when I tell someone my gig was canceled because of bad weather, or was double-booked, so I lost money. Inevitably someone will ask, why don't you get your gigs put on a contract? I have come to realize that the most basic reason is that most bars and restaurants won't sign contracts. They want to reserve the right to cancel a musician for any reason at all, without any notice, and then not pay them. They understand that you're not going to spend the money to challenge them in court, and you're going to have to take the loss. They have even more leverage if there's not a lot of work where you live.

I live in a major city and by that, I mean there are over three million people in four counties. All of these people and places are within an hour to an hour and a half of my house. That means there are lots of bars and restaurants for me to perform in, and if I lose one it's okay. I don't like losing clients, and I strive not to let it happen, but it does happen every now and then. So if I had an argument with a bar owner over a contract, it wouldn't be the end of the world. But if I lived in a less populous area with fewer venues, that would make it harder to stand up for myself and back a contract.

The majority of gigs that I have booked myself are basically done with a handshake and a certain amount of trust that everything is going to work out. If I had to guess, I would say that 90% of the time it works out just fine. Traditionally, even if they don't like me and don't want to rehire me, they will still pay me for my time that day. They will just not book me anymore and I won't play there again. It also goes the other way — if I don't like them, I won't call them for more gigs. Either way, standard practice is you play the gig and you get your fee. Although contracts are a very professional way to do business, it is not the norm on the bar and restaurant scene.

Around 2005, I was living in Baltimore and playing at a bar in Annapolis, Maryland. I had a contract with them that I had typed up and printed at home. It was pretty basic stuff. Dates and times, the amount of money, etc. I added a cancellation clause that stipulated that something like 6 weeks out this would happen, 4 weeks out this would happen, 2 weeks out this would happen, canceling me the day of the gig would require full payment, etc.

The general manager signed my contract and we laid out 12 dates over a four-month period; the first date was in December. When I woke up on the day of the first gig of this contract, it was snowing. Later that day I loaded up and was getting ready for what was normally a 45-minute to 1-hour drive. I had a very reliable vehicle that could make it to the venue through the snowy weather. Just before I was to leave the house, my phone rang and it was the manager on duty at the restaurant in Annapolis. He explained to me that they were going to close for the night because most of their employees couldn't even get there because of the snowy and icy roads. I was very nice about it, and knew that I had to eat this gig because if I made them stand on the contract then I would lose all the other dates that were booked. They would most likely cancel them, and I wouldn't play any gigs at all.

Four months later, at the time of the end of the contract, I didn't have a cell phone and I was playing a gig in Pennsylvania. I ended up spending the night in Pennsylvania and driving straight to Annapolis for my next gig. This was in March and was the last of the 12 gigs on this contract. When I arrived at the restaurant, the whole dining room and bar were packed. I thought to myself that this was going to be a fun night. I said hi to the bartender and got an iced tea. He said, "I have to grab the manager because he's been trying to call you all day."

The manager on duty was a really nice guy; I had worked with him many times. He came out to meet me at the bar and explained that the Maryland University basketball game was being televised that night and the bar was packed to watch it. It was March, the NCAA tournament, and the Maryland University men's basketball team was very good that year. He explained that he couldn't have me play that night, and that he had called me several times throughout the day and left messages on my answering machine.

I told him where I was the night before and that I'd been driving for four hours to get there. Then I offered to play some before the game, play during half-time, and even play a little after the game. He didn't want to do any of these things; he just wanted to cancel the music part of the night. So I told him I had my contract in the van and I would go get my backpack. After I showed him the contract he said, "Give me a few minutes, I need to call my general manager and see what he says."

I waited about 10 minutes for him to come back out and tell me that he was going to pay me. He went back to the office and wrote me a check. Part of my pay for the evening was a meal, and he honored that as well. I ordered a beer and some food and I relaxed for a little bit. They had a Chesapeake

Chicken Sandwich that was awesome. It's like a normal grilled chicken sandwich with crab meat added to it as a topping.

There was a price for standing up for myself and my contract. They didn't book me again for six months, and it took a little bit of work on my end for me to get another gig there. They never wanted to sign a contract with me again. They also had two other locations that I played at, though, and nothing bad happened at either of those. In hindsight, I could have lost those gigs as well by holding them to a contract and I am thankful that I didn't lose three venues. Any bad blood dissipated after a little bit of time passed, and I worked with that company for several years.

I learned a valuable lesson about putting more than one date on a contract. Every date should have its own contract so that future gigs aren't tied to a possible cancellation. Also, sending out contracts four months in advance sometimes isn't a good idea if you have multiple contracts and multiple gigs involved with one venue. Because if you stand up for yourself over one, they may cancel others without any penalties. I think it was a learning experience for both me and the venue. There was another adjustment I made for myself, and that was getting a cell phone.

When people offer me the advice of putting my gigs on contract so that I won't be canceled, they are trying to help and thinking of my best interest, but as I said before, the simple fact is most bars and restaurants won't sign a contract for a musician. I think the best thing I can do with a manager or owner of a restaurant or bar is to text or email all the details and ask them to confirm. That at least gives me some form of written agreement between me and the venue, which really helps in case of a double booking or any other discrepancy when it comes to my fee. Sometimes just having the basics covered is more than enough.

When dealing with licensed and bonded agents, I never see the contracts they have with the clients. I also never see the insurance papers that they are required to provide to their clients. There are some contracts from agents that I do sign like a Hold Harmless form. This form relieves the venue of any responsibility if something were to happen to my equipment, like an electrical surge or rainstorm damage. The venue will also not let you play in their establishment if you don't sign this form.

In all honesty, the best use of a small contract for a Solo Acoustic Musician is when it comes to playing private parties or corporate events that you have booked for yourself. A basic contract will enable you to receive a deposit of half payment up front. This way you can ensure that you get something even if they cancel at the last minute.

Let's say a customer at one of your restaurant gigs approaches you and asks you to play a birthday party. If your normal rate is $200 for three hours and they want to reserve your time on a Saturday, then most musicians would say to upcharge them to $400. The strategy here is to email them all the basic details and require a $200 deposit immediately. This is to hold the date on your calendar for them. In the email, you should state clearly that if they cancel for any reason, they do not get the deposit back. This will ensure that you are making the $200 you would have made at a restaurant gig no matter what.

Hopefully, everything goes well and you play the private party and make the other $200 plus any tips you may receive. But if something happens and two hours before the gig, they decide to call you and cancel for any reason at all, you have protected yourself with an email agreement that they agreed to and paid a nonrefundable 50% deposit. The email is dated and time-stamped and can be used for official purposes if needed. Even if you have a conversation in person or on the phone and discuss all of the details, you should be taking notes or filling out a checklist and then sending an email to confirm all the details. Once they have confirmed and responded to the email and made the deposit to you by cash, check, PayPal, or Venmo, you can add it to your calendar and feel safe that you have done your job on the business side.

# BOOKING CHECKLIST

I have stressed being prepared for many situations on gigs in SAM 1 & 2. Here in SAM 3, our focus is on getting gigs and learning about how to navigate the interactions we have with managers, owners, and agents (venue representatives). One way to be successful in this situation is to be prepared and one way to be prepared is to practice or create a mock interview. Creating a checklist of information for each venue and a list of expected questions and answers will take you to another level.

This is better than just winging it in a conversation only to forget something and then later remember it. It's better to hash it all out as best you can in one communication instead of trying to go over all the details in dozens of text messages or emails. The point is to be organized, thorough, detailed, direct, and professional. Think about this: if you are the only musician who communicates with a venue this way, you will stand out as having your act together. Hopefully, it will gain you respect from prospective clients and help you get more gigs with them.

You can start with a venue checklist. Make a document folder on your computer, pad, or phone and fill it with various venue checklists. This is just a guide and of course, you can tailor each individual checklist if needed. You may think of something that you want to add to your checklist, but this is a starting point and should cover most of the basics.

- Name of venue -
- Website -
- Location (address or city/town name) —
- Phone number -
- Email -
- Type of venue (bar, restaurant, country club, casino, etc.) —
- Days of the week for music (i.e., Thursday, Friday, Saturday) —
- Time of day for music (i.e., evenings 6-9 or 7-11) —
- Venue Representative (Contact for booking) —
- Contact Title (manager, owner, entertainment director, agent, etc.) —
- Cell Phone number -
- Email -
- Pay scale (what do they tell you they pay) —
- Added extras (free or discounted food, $25 tab, etc.) —
- How do they pay you (cash, check, PayPal or Venmo, etc.) —
- When do they pay you (at the beginning or end of the gig, in the mail, after the invoice is received) —
- Do I need to send an invoice?
- Do I need to fill out a tax form? (1099, W9, etc.) —

- How far out on the calendar do they book? (next month, three months, six months, one year, etc.) —

- What kind of rotation do you keep? (once a month, six weeks, eight weeks, etc.) —

- Is there a load-in/load-out area? (stage door, back door) —

- Is there a band parking space? Where do I park my vehicle?

- Where do the musicians set up to play?

- Is the stage area inside or outside? (I consider any place I set up to be the stage area) —

- If outside...

- Is there more than one spot to set up? (an alternate spot inside to avoid weather cancellations)

- Is there a stage?

- Is there a roof over the stage area?

- Are there flaps or walls?

- Does it flood on the ground of the stage area?

- Do they require the musician to have entertainer's insurance? (this is an optional question that you don't have to ask)

You can choose to leave out anything you want and skip whatever questions don't fit your criteria for a gig. You can make the checklist your own and rearrange the order as well as the language in any way that you see fit. The point is to organize your thoughts into a series of questions and answers that will help you gather all the information you need. Then you can file each document into a folder and easily access it if you need to.

Once you have booked a gig, you may have a few more questions for the contact person.

Do you want me to send you a promo picture for your in-house promotion?

They should use your approved picture for online websites and social media accounts. I don't like it when a venue representative just takes a picture off my site or social media account. I have a specific promo shot that I like to use, and as the SAM I should initiate this part of the booking conversation to make sure they use my approved picture. It is also another way to stand out and be professional, because a lot of musicians forget to ask this question and provide a picture.

After you have created your checklist, you must also prepare to answer the questions that they will ask you. Having answers prepared and adjusting for each different place will help you navigate the conversation more easily.

There are a lot of things that are part of the music business that I'm very bad at. Organization, being on time - the stuff you need in order to function in the regular world.
—Daniel Caesar

Let's pretend we are calling or going to a restaurant with the express purpose of asking them for a gig. So let's make a list of questions that they might ask us and have some answers ready.

Before calling or walking into the venue, we should have knowledge of open dates on our calendars and maybe even bring it with us. If I go to a venue, I usually have my calendar in my car. That way, if the conversation goes really well and they want to book some dates, I can go to my van and grab it. If this happens, you need to position yourself so they can't see your calendar. You don't want them to see the fees you charge other venues or how many open dates you have available. My advice is to always have a physical calendar, because a phone can fail. I have known some Solo Acoustic Musicians who lost their phones or had them destroyed somehow and did not have a physical backup calendar. They lost all of their dates. Make sure you keep both.

The venue representative may ask us...

- How much do you charge?

- Where else do you play?

- Do you provide your own P.A. system?

- How much space do you need to set up?

- How much time do you need to set up?

- How loud are you?

- Do you have a following?

- Can you supply break music?

- Are you available on Sunday afternoons?

- Can you provide an invoice?

- Do you have PayPal or Venmo to receive payment?

- Do you have entertainer's insurance?
- Can you play country music? (Country music is a specific example of a genre for the sake of the question)
- Can you play blues music? (another example of a specific genre to make the point)
- Can you play traditional Irish songs?

You are a Solo Acoustic Musician and you are asking for money to play music in a venue. What are your answers to these potential questions? Do you have answers prepared? Do you know how much space you need or how loud you are?

Answering these questions quickly and hopefully favorably can help you get the gig. Having answers prepared will make you look confident and capable.

You can probably think of even more questions that a venue representative might ask you. Add to my list and organize your own list any way you want. Once again, the point is to be prepared for the conversation.

WHO ARE THESE PEOPLE?

The person in charge of hiring musicians for a venue could have one of many different titles. I am pretty sure you will encounter many of them when you are trying to book gigs. I have come to define the position and what it means to me. The title can change based on the venue or how I think it applies. I will also supply some hard definitions. At the end of the day, you can call the person who hires you whatever you want, or whatever they want to be called, but I want you to understand the differences. I will also add that in this book I use the term "Venue Representative" as an umbrella term. When I am thinking to myself or talking with other Solo Acoustic Musicians, this term is what I use to identify the person doing the booking and managing the calendar.

Manager - This person is most likely the general manager or part of the management team of a venue like a restaurant or a bar.

Owner - This person is usually the owner of the venue. The most common owner that you will deal with will be the owner of a restaurant or a bar.

Third Party Agent - This person does not work at the venue but handles their entertainment calendar. This person will likely be another local musician or a friend of the venue.

Agent - In my experience, a licensed and professional talent agent may take over the calendar for a venue and handle all of the live music bookings. They will also have the ability to book you for private events.

Here are some titles and definitions that I found in my online search.

Booking Agent - a person who arranges concert or club engagements for performers.

What does a booking agent do?

A booking agent works in the music industry to book performers for concerts, gigs, and other live music performances. They often schedule performances and negotiate with the artists directly or with booking representatives or producers to arrange terms of contract, dates, and fees.

How do booking agents get paid?

Agents rarely receive above 15 percent on any booking they make with a promoter. The general standard hovers between five and 10 percent. If a show or tour is paid in advance, the agent collects the money, takes his or her cut, then pays the artist or their team.

A talent agent finds jobs for actors, authors, broadcast journalists, film directors, musicians, models, professional athletes, screenwriters, writers, and other professionals in various entertainment or broadcast businesses.

Event Coordinator — a professional in the hospitality and event industry who plans and coordinates events.

Event management is the application of project management to the creation and development of small and/or large-scale personal or corporate events such as festivals, conferences, ceremonies, weddings, formal parties, concerts, or conventions.

What do Entertainment Managers do?

An entertainment manager is responsible for booking and supervising events for a corporation. They serve as a liaison between the booking entity and the performers. The role differs from an entertainment business manager, as they are working for the venue or corporation as opposed to the performers. In addition to working with corporations, they may also work with venues like parks, hotels, or lodges. Their responsibilities include finding entertainers, negotiating contracts, overseeing marketing efforts, and managing a team tasked with carrying out the event. Having experience working with talent agents and event management can significantly improve your job prospects.

Are you as confused as I am about the title and the job of the person you may need to talk to about booking a gig?

I just gave some fairly specific definitions, and yet they can be interpreted differently. I know many musicians who think about these terms and their definitions differently than I do. All of them kind of mean the same thing to me, after all, as I am "the talent."

Here is a list of titles that are basically the same thing, but each person defines their position for themselves. You may encounter any of these during a day of contacting venues. Knowing this information will prepare you and make it easier to adapt your sales pitch when you are trying to book a gig.

Booker, Booking Manager, Booking Director, Booking Agent

Music Booker, Music Agent, Music Director, Music Co-Ordinator

Entertainment Director, Entertainment Coordinator,

Entertainment Manager, Entertainment Booker

Talent Agent, Talent Booker, Talent Director, Talent Manager

Event Director, Event Coordinator, Event Manager

Activities Director - This is one that I am encountering at every ALF (Assisted Living Facility) that I contact, so for me it is the title that I associate with that specific type of gig.

VENUE REPRESENTATIVE INTERVIEWS

I. DAVID NOVAK

Harbor Master Tiki Bar and Grill, Seminole, FL
12 noon - Wednesday, July 20th, 2022

My first stop on a quest to learn more about what the other side of the transaction thinks about booking Solo Acoustic Musicians brings me about thirty-five minutes south from my house to see my friend David Novak. I have known David for more than ten years and I even play music at his bar. As I drive there, I am thinking about how hot it is outside and wondering if I will need to use one of my gig fans during the interview.

I am looking forward to sitting down and hearing his point of view about everything he thinks about when booking a SAM. I am hoping to learn something new that I can share with you.

We are at Harbor Master Tiki Bar and Grill in Seminole, Florida, and it is a beautiful day to sit out by the water where the boats launch in and out. It is located at the Bay Pines Marina and it is noon. David has been the manager of this venue for a year. Before that, he was the general manager of another restaurant with two locations. David managed the music calendar for both spots for 14 years, booking performers for Wednesdays through Sundays.

David tells me that Harbormaster is a beer and wine bar. They also have a food menu, on a big chalkboard to the left when you enter the restaurant. I have seen people gather around to read it and make their decision. I have even seen people use their phones to take a picture of the chalkboard and then sit down to read the menu. There is a drink menu on another chalkboard on the right side, a little farther into the dining area.

Because it is at the marina, it is a fisherman's type of gathering spot where people come in off the boats and out of the sun and into the shade and want a cold beer and a sandwich. The location also makes this a hidden gem of a place. It is not on a main road, and it is behind a residential neighborhood. We are only two to three miles from the beach. It is a destination, and you must know where it is. The regular customers take pride in bringing new people here to hang out.

I know David is a busy guy, so I jump right in with my questions. He tells me that there are currently at least ten musicians on his roster. He hires musicians on Friday, Saturday and Sunday, and they typically play here once or twice a month. He hires solo and duo acoustic musician acts. He tells me that they play beachy types of music, and they are musicians that play at the beach. This makes sense to me because if you came here, you would feel the Jimmy Buffett vibe of the place and get a variety of pop and rock from different decades, depending on the musician. While they each may have a few different songs up their sleeve, they share a chill, laid-back attitude. That reminds me of a famous Jimmy Buffett saying, "change your latitude."

The musicians have a dedicated spot that is just inside the entrance of the Tiki Hut on the right. David revealed to me that he would like to build a little stage in that corner and that it is part of his plans for this venue. During his fourteen years at the previous venue, which had two locations, there was also a specific spot for the musicians. Both venues had a covered spot for the musician at an outside patio bar. He required each musician to bring an extra speaker to place just inside the door of the dining room. I always thought this was unique, and it worked out well because when I would play at this venue, I would make extra tips from the people dining inside. They could hear me and would either make a special trip out to tip me and make a request, or they would tip me on the way out of the venue after their meal.

At this point in this venue, David has given control of the calendar over to one of the local musicians. He still retains the final approval of each booking, though. The musician in control of the calendar is a friend of mine — I interviewed him in SAM 2. There are two reasons that I am interviewing David and not Jimmy. The first is that David has sixteen years of experience booking musicians between two different venues and still has the final say on who becomes a part of the roster. The second is that I interviewed Jimmy in SAM 2 as a Solo Acoustic Musician and he just started managing the schedule a couple of months earlier.

When Jimmy took over the calendar, he immediately brought in musicians he knew. As things progress, he will be dealing with musicians he does not know. David tells me that he gives everybody a shot for a gig. When somebody comes into the Tiki Bar, asks to talk to the manager and tells David that they are a musician, he will take their information and check out their online stuff — their website or social media links or a YouTube video. He will then pass their name on to Jimmy and tell him to put them on the schedule. He will give them a shot and after they play once, decide if he wants to hire them again. David has his own opinion on whether some-one is a good musician, but he also pays attention to how the customers react and he values his employees' opinions.

David is always on-site in the tiki bar and as the boss, he spends a great deal of time there. He has years of experience booking musicians and he watches all the new acts that they try out. Things he focuses on are what songs they play, how loud they are, and how they engage the audience.

He tells me that instead of calling or emailing the restaurant, he really prefers that musicians come to see him in person. David does not require an audition and does not believe in free auditions; he prefers to give somebody a paid gig and see how they do. If they do a respectable job, he will find them a spot in the rotation, and if they do not do a decent job or people do not seem to like them, at least they got paid for that day and it is no big deal. I interjected that this was a very fair proposal, because other places do not do it like that. At least you get a shot at displaying your skills, and you still get paid for your time.

As we were talking, we came to the topic of having a following. David shared with me an experience where a SAM brought a following of about twenty friends who came in, rearranged tables and took over a good part of the dining room. They ordered waters and stayed for the whole four hours of their friend's gig. He went on to say that they were continuously rude to the wait staff. That was on top of the fact that they took over a whole section and they were not buying food or drinks, so they were not tipping or spending any money at all. They had a generally negative attitude.

From the perspective of the musician, this can be confusing. Many venues want musicians to advertise and tell their friends and try to bring people to hear them play. It is eye-opening to hear a manager say that it can be counterproductive. That is what this book is for though, to try to share what the person who hires us is thinking and explore how the business side of being a gigging SAM works. The scenario that David described backfired on the musician. By bringing twenty friends who were taking up space without spending money and, in this case, even being rude, the musician alienated themselves from the venue and did not get hired back. It is important to make a note of this. If a venue asks you if you have a following, this is not what they want. What they want is for you to bring in people who spend money, who are nice, and who can have a fun time.

As a musician, I cannot control how people in the audience act. Sometimes it might be better to not have a following and to play at a busy place. If the venue has a regular crowd that is already having an enjoyable time, then my job as a SAM is simply to engage that audience and have fun with them. By showing up and entertaining them, I will create a following of the people that go to that venue on a regular basis. In the previous story, the musician might have been served very well by just showing up to play and not bringing friends. Then they might have been able to keep playing there and have a new venue on their calendar.

On the other side of the coin, and a completely opposite example, is a musician that David hires who lives more than an hour north of the venue. This guy used to live locally, near the beach where we are sitting and having our conversation. Back in the '70s and '80s, he was even in a local band that was extremely popular. Nowadays he plays solo acoustic shows, and he comes to the Harbormaster Tiki Bar once a month. He still has a following of friends who have loved him and his music for all these years. So when he puts the word out that he is coming to town, all his friends make it a point to put it on their calendars. This creates an event atmosphere and even adds an element of a homecoming reunion or a friendly family get-together. All these people show up to have an enjoyable time, listen to music, and buy food and drinks.

When added to an already busy weekend evening scene happening in the venue, it becomes quite a fun time. It has even become a special monthly thing for those people who want to come and hear their friend play music.

I finally got to ask David why he would fire someone or not rehire them, and here are his thoughts.

He says the first thing he does not like is unprofessionalism. After that, he added that being on time for the gig was important. Then he mentioned bump music. I was not familiar with this term, but he meant the break music between the performer's sets. He wants the musician to be able to provide break music.

Bumper music, or a bump, is a term used in the radio broadcasting industry to refer to short clips of signature songs or theme music used to buffer transitions between programming elements, typically lasting no longer than fifteen seconds.

He does not like dead air between the house music and the live music, so he wants a quick and easy transition between them. He says that a lot of musicians take way too much time between when they are done playing and turning on their break music. He does not think they realize how long the dead air is, and says that the audience should never have that dead space between music. He compares it to a radio program and how they move in and out of songs. He's looking for a good flow.

David also says that he would not rehire someone if they were rude to his staff. He tells me that in his experience some musicians can be pompous and arrogant. He made an example of asking one musician to turn down the volume and their response was, "No I'm not going to turn it down." Then David tells me about a musician who took an hour-long break. He looked at me almost shocked and said, "I don't know where the guy went." I asked him for clarification, and he expressed that a normal break would be 15 to 20 minutes every hour, but disappearing for a whole hour was unacceptable.

David also explained that some musicians will take advantage of a bar tab. He told me that not all his musicians get a bar tab as part of their deal, but that some do get food and drinks as part of their pay. Now remember, David has been booking musicians for somewhere around sixteen years at this point and has seen a lot of shenanigans. He recalls an example of a musician ordering fifteen beers and expecting him to comp that bar tab as part of their pay. I will be honest, this sounds like an exaggeration to me, but in all the years he has been doing this it is quite possible that a musician ordered and drank that many beers. Either way, he says reasonable is reasonable and that the musician should not take advantage of the situation.

David shifts the conversation to how he likes to deal with a cancellation or a musician needing to call off a shift. He tells me that he prefers the musician to try and hopefully be able to get someone to cover the shift. He also says that at this point he does have Jimmy managing the calendar and that having him try to cover the shift also helps. In all of his years at the previous venue, he didn't have that buffer and he explains to me that it is not fun, as a manager who may have a busy dinner service happening, could be short-staffed in the kitchen, or wait staff, and could be dealing with unhappy customers, to then have a musician call out sick at the last minute, an hour before they're supposed to start. As a manager who likes to have music consistently in his venue, this means he must stop all the other stuff he is doing and try to call a bunch of musicians to find one available at the last minute. He says the last thing he wants to worry about is whether his musician is showing up or not.

Another scenario that rarely but sometimes happens is a musician calling the bar to tell someone that they cannot make it, and David says that they should have called him or Jimmy to plan to have someone cover their shift. He also adds that they should make sure that not only Jimmy, who is the one in charge of the calendar now, but also he himself has their phone number and email on file.

When I asked David how he manages double bookings he looked at me and asked, "Why would that happen?" He explains that it has rarely ever happened and that if it did, it was a mistake made by the musician with their calendar. His policy is that the musician who is on his calendar is the one who plays the gig. At least he has a protocol in place and knows what to do if the situation arises. I have encountered other venue managers who did not know what to do when it happened. I would like to think that a musician would not make this mistake and put something on their calendar without confirmation, but I have seen it happen. Even I recently showed up to play a gig and another musician arrived while I was setting up. After a conversation with the manager, it became clear that the other musician must have misunderstood an email. I continued setting up and played the gig because I was the one booked on the venue's calendar.

Right now, David is booking four-hour spots three evenings a week. Friday and Saturday nights are from 4:30 to 8:30 PM and Sundays are from 4 to 8 PM. This fall, the Tampa Bay Buccaneers will be playing four o'clock games and David will be canceling music on those Sundays because the locals want to watch the game. Harbormaster Tiki is not a late-night place and closes around 9 or 10 PM depending on the night of the week, so it only has dinnertime music shifts.

I bring up the topic of weather protocols. This is a tiki bar on the water, but it has a wide area covered by a roof and there are flaps to put down all around the outside walls. David tells me that if a rainstorm comes up, we as musicians can pause to make sure everything is going to be okay. He also adds that he thinks the musician's equipment should be up off the ground a little bit. Like a speaker on a stand. He tells me he can provide egg crates if the musician needs them to lift something up because he does not want their gear to get wet. He says that he even has tarps if the musician needs them. Another point he makes is that if it rains for half an hour and the musician pauses, when the musician can resume playing they will still stop at their scheduled end time, and he will pay them in full. It is just weather and something with which we must deal.

An interesting story came up during our talk and it is important to share it. When David first opened this bar a year ago, the owner did not give him any money for a music program. A local musician approached him to play there, and he explained that he did not have any money to pay him. The musician then agreed to play for free so that he could invite other managers and owners of other venues to come to hear him play, in hopes of getting gigs at other places. At some point, David was able to talk the owner into giving him a music budget, so he started to hire musicians and pay them. So when this musician who had been playing for free finished one night, David offered to pay him for the gig and explained to him that now he was hiring musicians.

According to David, this musician got very mad and started yelling at him. The guy was angry that David was now paying musicians! Then the guy argued about the fee that David was willing to pay him and said that it was $50 less than the going rate around town. David explained that this was the budget he had and that he was trying to pay the man for his services. The guy got very upset and was screaming and yelling, acting like he wanted to fight David. He was calling him names as he walked out of the Tiki Bar. The guy even yelled that he was going to tell everyone that this place sucked and that David was a horrible manager.

I listened very intently, and this is my take on the situation. The musician agreed to play for free and he also used it for a purpose of trying to book gigs in other venues. Then when this venue offered to pay him, instead of being grateful and understanding that he had earned a spot on the roster, he got mad and said it was not enough money. Making the situation even worse, he started to yell and insult the manager who was trying to do right by him and pay him from now on and give him gigs. I am quite sure at this point that guy has burned his bridge with David.

If you think about it this situation is confusing. Initially, the musician came in asking for money to play a gig. The manager did not have any music budget and yet the musician agreed to play for free. It was the musician's idea. After months went by, things changed, and the manager was now able to pay the musician, but instead, the musician got mad and stormed out. It just does not make any sense to me that he reacted that way. I believe he should have been grateful for the upgrade from free to paid. Also, he was using the venue to audition for other bookers, and to get gigs at other venues. He had created a useful spot for himself at this venue until he got mad. He created an opportunity and then self-sabotaged it. David is a loyal guy and I think he would have hired him for a long time on a regular basis and paid him from then on. That guy just threw away a steady client and stream of gigs. I have never heard a story like this in all my years.

David is still at work the day we talk, and I am grateful that he has carved out a little bit of time to sit and talk with me about his experience booking musicians. We are interrupted a couple of times by some of his regular patrons who come over to say hi and talk to him for a minute. I have been expecting this to happen, and it is cool with me. David is being gracious enough to bless me with his knowledge and I am thankful for his time. A representative from Great Bay Beer distributors also comes in with new promotional signs for a beer special they are selling. David asks him to check on keg temperatures and things like that and they chat about business for a minute.

In hindsight, I really wish a musician had showed up to give him a sales pitch while I was sitting there at the table. That would have made for a great addition to this book!

David explains to me that he thinks a SAM should visit the venue before they approach someone about booking a gig. We decide to call it a scouting mission. He says they should scout it out before they go, because not every venue is a good fit for them. The previous venue he booked was an upscale restaurant and they wanted people to turn over tables. This means that they wanted people to have a nice dinner and drinks and then leave, because they had people waiting to get a table. But here at the Tiki Bar, he wants people to stay and have an enjoyable time and spend money. So he thinks it is important for a SAM to know the venue where they are going to be trying to play, even going as far as to know who the manager or bartender is before they approach anyone. He cites an example of one musician who came and repeatedly asked him about playing there, but this was before he was able to pay musicians. He does hire that guy now that he can pay him. He tells me that that guy would come in and have food and drinks, and that he was a patron.

He continues by saying that you need to have good videos on your website, or a link to your YouTube page. He adds that when he asks a musician if they have a video on YouTube, it should be on their business card because he has had musicians ask for a pen and write it down on the back of their cards. He says it is your job to be prepared for an interview to get a gig. Another thing he says is to make sure the manager is not busy, and to come to the restaurant at a slower time when you finally do approach them about playing their venue. David shares that he knows managers or owners will brush people off and say they are too busy. He tells me that he tries to talk to everybody so that he can hopefully give them a chance.

Following up with a phone call is particularly important. David says that he cannot believe how many times a musician will meet him, talk for a minute, and leave a business card, and then he never hears from them again.

If you get a gig from David, he does not want you to use one of his chairs for your tip can. He thinks it is more professional if you have your own merchandise table to hold your tip can or CDs or whatever you have for promotion, including business cards. He makes sure to tell me that the musician should confirm all the details of the gig: the money you are being paid for the gig, including if your payment has a tab for food and drinks, and the time you are supposed to perform.

One thing David talked about that I think is unique is placing a judgment on booking someone based on their phone number area code. Where we live in Florida is very transitory and full of tourists and vacation people. We have what we call snowbirds who come here for four to six months of the year. And we have people that visit for three months to a year and a half and then leave. So when a new musician approaches David and he does not have a local phone number, it sticks out to him.

He had a bit of advice for people trying to get a gig when they have just moved to a new town or even a new state. He told me I could sign up for Google Voice, which would allow me to pick any area code I wanted and create a Google phone number. Then I could give this number to booking contacts at venues and it would have a local area code. When someone called that number, it would go straight to my phone, and it was free. I like this idea because it is a solution to an often-overlooked potential problem. As a musician who moved to Florida fifteen years ago, I only waited a few months to change my phone number because I thought I was losing callbacks because of my out-of-state phone number. I do not have any solid proof of that, but once I changed to a local area code, I received more return calls about gigs. I surely do not think it would hurt to try this tactic if you are new somewhere.

You as a SAM may not need to use the Google Voice idea for booking. Especially if you have lived in the same area for a long time and you are established. But you could share this idea with a friend who is moving out of your area to somewhere new, or with someone who is new to your area. Also, if you know someone who is going to visit somewhere for a few months, then you might want to give them a heads-up about something that might help them get gigs.

David notices when musicians set up quickly and break down their equipment quickly and efficiently. One of the things that annoys him is when a musician takes a long time to break down and load out. If a musician's gig is over at 8:30 PM and the bar closes an hour later, and the SAM is not finished loading out, David does not like that. He goes as far as to say that he might not hire somebody back if that is an issue. I have seen musicians end their gigs and then go to the bar for forty-five minutes to an hour to drink beers and talk to people before ever starting to pack up and load out at all. That is the kind of thing he is talking about.

I always pack up and load out quickly, and if I want to hang out and talk to people, then I do it after that. It is a good rule to stick by and when David told me that, it just confirmed what I thought was the right thing to do. He told me that he has had to have his employees help someone load out because they were trying to close the doors and go home, and the musician was still not finished packing up their gear.

David ends the interview by saying one last thing: "Don't play 'Sweet Caroline.' I am sick of hearing that one."

We end our chat a little before 1 PM and I head toward the beach to take a slow way home, hoping I've captured useful tips for fellow SAMs. I have plans to stop at a couple of places on the way to talk to people about gigs and drop off my card. I also have my swimsuit and will stop off for a swim, and then sit in my beach chair to think about our interview.

I will see David again in a couple of weeks when I show up to play my gig at Harbor Master Tiki Bar and Grill.

II. SYLVIA TZEKAS

Sea Sea Riders, Dunedin, FL
2 PM – Thursday, August 4th, 2022

It was another lovely yet hot day here in Florida and I headed a few miles from home into downtown Dunedin. It is a small town on the intercoastal of the west coast of Florida and Sea Sea Riders is right at the center of it all. Located on the western end of the main street strip it is only steps from the marina and the daily sunsets on the water. You can sit on the wrap-around porch to enjoy the sunset with dinner and drinks. Dunedin has a rich history and a vibrant downtown scene but that is a whole different book that someone else has already written. Our focus today is on Sylvia, her restaurant, and the music.

Sea Sea Riders is in a vibrant downtown area and there is a lot of foot traffic. The weekends can be especially busy with people on the sidewalks making their way to the shops and restaurants that line the main street. We talk about the differences in town since she started having music and observe that there are more than forty new restaurants, bars, and breweries that have opened in that time. The downtown area has become a destination for locals in the Tampa Bay area as well as tourists who are visiting Florida.

The name of the restaurant is a play on words, between seafood and the song. The location close to the water also had an impact on choosing the name. When I asked her about the song and which version influenced her, she was quick to say Mitch Ryder and the Detroit Wheels. Their version came out in 1966. During this part of our conversation, she told me to learn one of the versions. She added that most of the musicians on her roster play a version of the song. I was honest with her when I said I didn't know the other musicians were doing that. I think it could be fun to give it a shot. Sylvia told me that there were more than a hundred recorded versions of the song and that it is one of the most covered songs ever. She did know the history of the song and was correct that Ma Rainey was the original performer in 1924. I guess I have homework for the next time I play music at Sea Sea Riders.

Sylvia is a busy business owner who splits her time between family, the restaurant, and taking an active role in her community. She donates her time and resources to charitable local events and is well known by other local business owners. Her restaurant is successful and has some awards to validate that. With a couple of award-winning cocktail drinks on the menu, Sea Sea Riders have also recently won a "Best Seafood Restaurant" award in Tampa Bay. I think the old house built around 1900, which has become a local favorite dining destination, has an old Florida feel that people enjoy.

We grab a corner booth at the end of the main dining room and sit down to talk. Sylvia has owned the restaurant since 1988 and started hiring Solo Acoustic Musicians about fifteen years ago. She tells me that she noticed other local restaurants and bars downtown having music and thought it was a good idea to do the same thing. When I first started playing music here, the whole layout was different. About six years ago, they did a massive renovation project and made some major changes to the floorplan. The musicians used to play in the corner of the small lounge area and now they have a dedicated corner in a much larger dining room that has a rectangular U-shaped bar in the middle.

I reminded Sylvia about the first time she asked me to bring an extra speaker to put outside. I told her that was the first time anyone had asked me to do that, and I didn't like the idea in the beginning. But I remember when some friends heard me two blocks away at the gas station and came and found me to have drinks and listen to me play. It was then that I thought she had a good idea for bringing in customers.

Each Solo Acoustic Musician she hires can bring their normal PA, but she also wants a speaker on the outside porch aimed at the street to draw in foot traffic. She says, "As people are walking by, they hear the music and they come into the restaurant." This idea came from a personal experience she had one evening when she walked out of her house. She lives down a residential street but at the one end of the street is another street that has restaurants and bars on it. As she walked outside, she could hear someone singing in the distance. This led to her and her husband walking down the street to find the musician and they decided to have a drink and listen to some songs. She thought it was a great idea to add this to her own restaurant.

The topic of weather almost seems unnecessary because the musicians play inside. But we still have to talk about the speaker that goes outside. Sylvia tells me that some SAMs put a trash bag over their speaker and some of them place it under the roof of the wrap-around porch. I also note that stopping the gig for a minute and bringing the speaker in during a rainstorm is another option, and I know from experience that Sylvia is comfortable with all three. It is about teamwork and what makes everyone involved safe and happy. After all, the outdoor speaker is meant to draw in people who are walking down the street and during a complete downpour there is no one outside. As soon as it stops raining, the musician can put their extra speaker right back on the porch again to maximize its use.

Sylvia currently has about twelve Solo Acoustic Musicians on her roster. She is using those musicians in rotation to fill three shifts a week. Friday and Saturday nights from 6 to 10 PM and Sunday afternoons from 1 to 5 PM. She only hires Solo Acoustic Musicians, and she likes to have a variety of genres represented. Her desire to mix it up brings in jazz, blues, folk, and rock artists. She also has a balance between male and female performers, which adds to the diversity of the song choices that are being made by the musicians. Overall, she wants to provide a variety of music to keep it fresh and interesting for her patrons.

When I ask her about her preference for how a musician approaches her about booking a gig, she explains that she likes to receive a social media message on the restaurant's page and that she also prefers that the musician come to the restaurant in person to introduce themselves. I would think it would be common sense, but she makes sure to tell me it is important to be polite and nice when asking to talk with her. It is also important to give her a business card and allow her time to check out the links to your website and videos. She adds that she doesn't like it when a musician comes to the restaurant every week repeatedly and that it becomes a little bit "stalky." Her advice is to not be obsessive. It is good to do follow-ups with her, but do them at the right time and not too frequently. She shares with me that some of the musicians are like stalkers and that if they see her car in the parking lot, they will come into the restaurant to press her about booking a gig.

As we talk, a thought crosses my mind and I ask Sylvia if she thinks this is because of her location and the proximity to a lot of other bars and restaurants that have live music.

She agrees that it's possible that musicians come to downtown Dunedin and work their way up the street so that they could talk to people in, let's say, twenty different venues. I had never thought of it like that before, but she is not isolated, and the downtown area is a very popular destination. It probably leads to a lot of musicians coming in looking for work all the time.

Part of the reason she likes to meet the musician in person is to get a sense of their personality. Some of the musicians might be good players, but their personalities might not fit her venue. She also tells me that she likes the musician to have a video and a YouTube link that they can send her in a social media message. Her reasoning is that it's very easy for her to just click on the link and not have to go look for someone. Doing this will make it more likely that she will listen to their music. Sylvia tells me that if a musician includes some of their other dates, and they are nearby, that she will try to go hear them play some songs. She will look at their website and check their calendar to see what other kinds of places they are playing. By doing all these things she can get an idea of whether they would be a good fit for her restaurant.

I ask her if there is an ideal time of day that someone should call her or come talk to her in person. Her answer was immediate. Midday. Do not call or stop in at 6:30 PM during dinner service. Sylvia says that musicians do that a lot. She adds that sometimes they stop into the restaurant in person in the middle of a dinner rush on a Friday evening and want to talk to her about booking music. I have to say that I can understand why this would be annoying to a business owner. I can also tell you that I have advised other musicians not to do it, because the manager or owner of the venue will remember you for the wrong reason. I even tell Sylvia that if

I was the owner of a bar and oversaw booking the music, I would wonder why the musician wasn't playing a gig on Friday night. If they were a good musician, they would probably be booked somewhere and not bothering me during a busy dinner service on the weekend. She smiles at my perspective, and I think maybe she has never heard it from that point of view before but that it makes sense to her as an owner who hires musicians.

As we were talking, a man walked in and approached the hostess station. Sylvia paused to tell one of her employees to see what the man needed, and apologized to me for the interruption. I think it was a vendor, not a customer. I told her that I expected that to happen during our talk because she is still running a business, after all, and I am on her time today.

I asked her why she continues to hire a musician. What I mean is, once they get a gig here, why would she continue to hire them once or twice a month for a long time? Sylvia is on-site a lot and she pays attention to what's going on. She is quick to tell me that she listens to her customers, and that they will tell her if they like the musician or if they don't. Even on her own, she is paying attention to the crowd's reaction to the musician. She explains to me that they are first a restaurant and then a bar, and that the music must complement the environment. Adding that she wants to make sure the acoustics and the volume levels are appropriate because people are dining and having conversations and it's not all about the music. She wants to make sure there is a good balance between the music and the patrons.

There are times in the restaurant when the crowd is a little rowdier and the musician can be a little louder, and there are times when the customers are more interested in a quiet dinner and the musician needs to turn down a little. It's nice to have the music there, and her guests love it, but sometimes they are just looking to have some conversation and not be overwhelmed by loud music. She looks for musicians that can tell the difference throughout the gig and change with the audience. She pays attention to how a musician reads the crowd's response. She gave examples of a group of people who were responsive and talkative with the musician, and then the opposite: a group of people who wanted to be left alone. Her expectation is that the musician be able to tell the difference quickly and adjust to the guests in front of them.

Sylvia also has a core of employees who have been there a long time and she values their opinions about the musicians she hires. I am sure they all have their own favorites but I'm also pretty sure that they are all objective when listening to the musicians. When she hires a new musician at Sea Sea Riders, she will approach different members of the staff during their first gig and ask for their opinions about the music.

I turned the conversation to the opposite side, and asked her why she would fire someone or not hire them again. Again, her first response went right to the customers; she said that if a musician isn't paying attention to what the guests want, that is bad. Secondly, she returned to the volume question and said that if the musician is too loud and aggressive and it seems like it's all about themselves, that doesn't work very well in her venue. She doesn't want to see her bartenders and waitstaff having to scream or raise their voices to talk to the customers. Once again there's a need for balance because it's really about everyone in the room having an enjoyable experience. Thirdly, she states that she pays attention to their attitude and how they interact with her staff. She tells me that she has hired some musicians who are super demanding and needy. Everyone should be working together and getting along without diva rockstar attitudes in the mix.

The word "obnoxious" appeared in our conversation and we explored that topic further. She said if the musician is arrogant, she doesn't care how good they are at music. She says, "We've had a few that were super arrogant and basically just downright rude. Even to the customers." She continued speaking as if she was one of those musicians and said, "This is what I'm playing, this is how I'm playing it; if you don't like it tough." Believe it or not, she has asked a musician to pack up and leave after his first set, saying he was arrogant and absolutely rude. I asked her if she paid him, and she told me that she paid him to go away. Telling him to pack up his stuff and just go. I don't think this happens very often in her venue and she told me that this had been about 10 years ago. This musician must have been really over the top and a jerk to rub everyone there so wrong. In my opinion, one of the easiest parts of this lifestyle is to just be nice to people. Clearly, that musician did not get the memo.

Sylvia insists that performers be on time for their gigs. She had to let a musician go once because he was repeatedly arriving at the venue fifteen minutes after his scheduled start time. She told me she liked his music, and he was a nice person, but he was constantly late to his shift. She hired him several times, but it just didn't work out.

Since we were discussing time management, Sylvia brought up the topic of set breaks. There is a time we start the gig and a time we end the gig, and in between the musician will take a few breaks. As a musician, I know that in my mind I have a schedule of how I'm typically going to do things when I am on a gig. She gives an example of a musician playing a set when there are not very many people there and then not recognizing that during their last song, a whole lot of people came in, and then they go on break. I know exactly what she is talking about. Sometimes I must call an audible, like a football quarterback changing the play at the line of scrimmage, and just keep playing on for another half hour before I take a break. In the specific case of Sea Sea Riders restaurant, it might be because the speaker I have outside has drawn foot traffic into the restaurant to hear me play. If I then go on break right as a bunch of people come in, they might not stick around at all, which defeats the purpose of having the speaker outside. She explains that she knows musicians need to take breaks because of their voices and their fingers getting tired, but her emphasis is on knowing when to stay on stage a little longer. She suggests maybe playing a shorter set when it's kind of slow to balance out the possibility of playing a longer set when things get busier. I will be honest and add that I am happy to hear an owner have some empathy for the musician about the need to take a break, and to have the foresight of knowing that the crowd can change over a four-hour gig and the musician may need to change their break schedule accordingly.

Another part of taking a break is turning on music. Sylvia is okay with the musician providing music for their breaks or turning on the house music. Each musician has a different approach to this. Personally, I like the mix of music that this venue plays when I am on break, and it just works for me to go that route. I know for a fact that one of the jazz musicians that Sylvia hires puts on his own break music so that it's consistent with his performance. He likes to keep the music all jazz when he is there working. I can agree with this approach and having a designated musical format all the way through his time in the venue.

She also doesn't like it when someone calls off a gig at the last minute. I ask her what her policy is in that situation. She tells me it's not a big deal if someone needs to cancel and they give her plenty of notice because then she can book somebody else. She understands that sometimes there can be an emergency, but as a rule, she's looking for consistency with her musicians. She also said that if the musician wants to call some of the other musicians from her roster that they know already play there and try to find a replacement, she encourages that. If they can't find a replacement, then she will call musicians she knows and approves of already. She adds that sometimes she will reach out to someone who is trying to play there and give them a chance as a last-minute fill-in. I see this as an opportunity for that musician. If they are available that night and they can do the gig, maybe they will get on the roster. I can say from personal experience that I have landed quite a few new clients in the past by covering for someone else who canceled. The most important thing to note is that the musician who needs to cancel should not just send a replacement that Sylvia doesn't know. Communication is vital to the process in this situation.

When I ask Sylvia about how she handles a double booking she replies that thankfully, that situation does not happen very often. She will make sure to give the musician who is canceled and does not play that day priority on the upcoming calendar, booking an extra replacement date for them where she can fit it in. Sylvia will also make sure to comp them a meal, and she is honestly apologetic if a double booking happens. I am empathetic and understand that although we don't want it to happen, mistakes do occur from time to time. Sometimes it is the owner's fault and sometimes it is the musician who gets mixed up. It is just a part of the equation to be prepared for in the life of a Solo Acoustic Musician.

Sylvia likes the musicians to promote their gigs at her venue and to tell their fans and friends when they're going to be there. The restaurant has a few social media pages, and they post about live music along with their dinner and drink specials or other events. Since I mentioned dinner specials, I will add that Sylvia also provides a meal as part of the musician's pay.

With a stable roster of around twelve musicians, Sylvia can and will book her calendar at least six months in advance. As one of her musicians, I know that I booked January through June, and then eventually we did July through December. I play here once a month as part of the rotation. We are in the first week of August when we sit for this interview, and her calendar is full through the end of the year. I would expect her to start to book into the New Year's calendar sometime around late October. She tells me she likes to do it like that so she can just take care of it and not have to deal with it again for a while.

In addition to the local Solo Acoustic Musicians that Sylvia hires on a regular basis, she also is open to hiring people from out of town who are visiting. The part of Florida that we live in has multiple tourist seasons, and some of the people that visit are musicians. SAMs from many other states come to Florida for a week or up to several months at a time. She likes to be able to provide a visiting SAM with a gig, and some of them do very well and even make it an annual thing. It works out for everybody, because the musician can invite their family and friends who live here to hear them play in her restaurant. It is good for her business, and it is good for the musician to have a place to play. She explains that they usually come to town and come to the restaurant to have lunch or a midday drink with family or friends. Then at some point, they might approach her about playing a gig while they're in town.

As our conversation was winding down, Sylvia confided to me that she really likes it if musicians want to play in her restaurant. She knows it's a paid gig, but she doesn't want it to be just about the money. She thinks that if the musician likes her venue and enjoys being there, versus having to be there because they must make a certain amount of money on their monthly calendar, they will perform better.

As soon as we finished talking, Sylvia thanked me and disappeared into the kitchen. She always has a lot to do, so I am sure she had something important to attend to. I am grateful for her sharing some of her valuable time and wisdom with me. After our chat, I had to drive down to the beach and play a birthday party at a local yacht club. On my drive, I reflected on our conversation and thought to myself that it was fun to sit with someone who has been booking me to play music for more than ten years and to hear her thoughts on the business. I hope that you, the reader, will gain something from my experience today.

III. JANE MCKEE

Season's 52, Tampa, FL
2 PM – Tuesday, August 9th, 2022

Today I am driving over to Tampa, about an hour from home. I have chosen a nice restaurant that I have been to before in hopes that a booth will be a quiet place to sit and talk. Even at 2 PM, it's busier than I expected, and I check in while I wait for Jane to arrive. I use the extra time to gather my thoughts before our conversation. I have known Jane for several years and I even work with her in a musician/agent relationship. I'm excited to learn more about her and her company. Jane arrives shortly after, and we are shown to our table.

I ask Jane for a little bit of background and how she got into being an agent. She tells me that in 1969 she was working for a Capitol Records distributor in Buffalo, NY. She was doing this when she was home in the summer while working on a master's degree in college there. During that summer she also went to the famous Woodstock concert in Bethel, NY. She says, "That turned my whole life around." Because of what she was doing with Capitol Records, she had a certain level of access. She adds that she thought she would never get backstage because her vehicle was so far back in the line of people on the road waiting to get to the site. Someone got hurt and the sheriff commandeered her vehicle. So because of that happening, she got backstage with her boss's truck, and that led to spending a few days at Bob Dylan's house. She was also hanging out with Crosby, Stills, and Nash during that time. She waited there until the traffic leaving town had died down considerably.

After she went back to the Buffalo, NY, area she finished her master's degree. As the summer ended, her boss sent her to meet up with Bob Seger and his band in mid-September. It was there that Jane met her first husband, who was the keyboard/saxophone player in the band, and this led her to move to Michigan. Jane tells me that there was a lot of traveling and big shows. Some of these tours in the Midwest included acts like the Monkees and Janis Joplin. After this part of her life ended, Jane moved to Florida in 1981, and in 1994, she began her journey to becoming an agent. With her previous experience and contacts, she found her way into the Tampa Bay music scene. Jane says that she was being approached by local bands asking her to manage them. She had spent many years as a teacher and was now splitting her time between the high school during the day and working with bands at night. This led her to retire from teaching in 1999 and focus strictly on being an agent. During those first five years, Jane was carving out a spot for herself. There were only two other talent agents in Tampa at the time, and she was able to establish herself with local musicians and venues. It was to become the foundation for growing her business to where it is today.

Jane is a licensed and bonded agent based in the Tampa Bay area, and the owner of her own company, Jane's World Entertainment. Her company has been a legitimate business for more than 26 years and has grown to where she has two agents on her staff. Jane's World doesn't deal with models, actors, films or authors, or those types of acts or performers. Her agency's focus is on music, and it handles all types of gigs, working with small to large venues. The musicians that she works with range from solos, duos, trios, and full bands from local areas to regional and national touring acts. Our focus today will be on how Jane interacts with Solo Acoustic Musicians. It has a lot to do with what the client wants and then hopefully she can provide them with a quality musical act.

She is also connected to production companies which would include things like staging, lighting, LED screen presentations, and all that kind of stuff. All these things are available through her company if a client wants to have a one-stop shop and put together an event. She has spent more than two decades working with the Tampa Bay Lightning, our professional hockey team, and the Tampa Bay Buccaneers, our professional football team. Jane's World has provided them with musicians and bands of all levels and even the full production items we listed earlier. These two professional sports organizations work with her on game days as well as many other events that they have throughout their seasons, including Hall of Fame induction ceremonies, an annual cancer fundraiser and benefit, and even providing staging for the ESPN commentators that visit the stadium during training camp.

Jane tells me that she works 24/7 and not because she must, but because it keeps her busy and she enjoys it. She adds that most booking agents don't have downtime. If they want to be successful, they must work all the time. Phone calls, text messages, and emails come in at all hours and from all over the country. One of her clients is the Hard Rock casino on the east side of Tampa and she tells me that next month she has bands coming in from Nashville, Las Vegas, and LA.

Jane explains to me that it is vital for a booking agent to know the legalities of being an agent. The reason she says this is that each state has different laws and rules for agencies to follow and one needs to know what they are. I would think it might be important for a Solo Acoustic Musician to know what they are as well. Part of having a career as a SAM is knowing things that are important in the business. Jane is very professional and wants her clients and her musicians to understand the contracts they are signing, to know what is expected of them, and what the venue is providing. Some of these arrangements can be complicated and that's why it's good to have the agent handle this part of the business.

According to Jane, Florida is stringent in its regulations for booking agents. But something they don't do at the Department of Business and Professional Regulations in Tallahassee, which is the state capital, is follow up properly on unethical agents. She says, "We have them in our area." (We are not going to name names or discuss this any further.) I will say to you, the reader, that you have to look out for people that are not running a professional honest business. All you can do is try to be aware of what's right and wrong and work with people that do what you think is proper. Avoiding working with a bad agent would be another good reason to learn the rules and laws that they must abide by in the state where you live. By a bad agent, I mean someone who will rip you off or treat you poorly and not do honest business.

I know you probably want me to explain more, and I will give you examples of someone not treating you correctly. There are stories about agents who will double dip. Jane explains that some agents will charge the venue and charge the musician to book a date. This is not ethically right. Another example she brings up is when an agent takes too large a percentage of the performance fee. There are music industry business books out there that will list typical rates in these areas. Depending on what type of agent they are and what kind of relationship they have with their musician or venue, an agent can make from 10% to 25%. Jane tells me she's pretty sure that there is information available with a rate of 10% to 20% in Florida. I know I wouldn't want an agent to take 50%

of my pay. Even if someone wanted to take 20% of my $200 gig, that would seem excessive. That would be $40. I do not think I would agree to that deal.

Jane likes to get to know the musicians that she's hiring on the local level. She doesn't like to just book random new people at her venues unless they come highly recommended by a musician she's been working with for a while. Or if a venue owner says, "Hey Jane, I want you to try this musician because they're really great." She used to go out on weekends a lot more and stop in at many venues and check out local solo acts and bands. But nowadays it's more about who approaches her and what kind of references they have. She doesn't have to hunt down good musical acts and has a good-sized roster to pick from as it is. When it comes to selecting artists to book, she tells me that a very important part of what she does is to do her homework on the musician.

One of Jane's venues which has been a regular client for 13 years has five locations presenting live music right now. They have had a few more locations in the past and are always looking to expand. Like most businesses, there's a certain amount of ebb and flow to their growth pattern. These venues are Irish-American-themed restaurant/bars, and they hire Solo Acoustic Musicians through Jane to provide live music. Most of the locations have a Thursday/Friday/Saturday music schedule. A couple of them do some Wednesday music and a couple of others do some Sunday music. Jane handles all of their calendars and is the liaison between the corporate office and the musicians. She must coordinate with all the musicians and deal with any cancellations or changes to the calendar that may occur.

Jane gives me a quick rundown of how she deals with a potential client who approaches her to book a musician for a one-time event. She will call and email SAMs and say, listen, I have this date open. Are you available? Then she will collect several people who are available that day and she will give them a period of time to await an answer, along with a possible budget. This is specifically for when it's not one of her regular clients. She will ask the client about money, to determine the best that they can do. She will ask the client for a high number, because she charges them a percentage as a fee. The more the musician makes, the more Jane makes, and she doesn't want to lowball anybody. If the musician is being paid $200, she charges the client 15%, so the client must pay $230. She does this instead of taking money from the $200 that the musician is making. I really like the way she handles this.

Jane states that communication between the musician and the agent needs to be clear. If an agent calls or emails and asks, "Are you open on a particular date?" but doesn't offer any other information, it doesn't help the musician decide how to respond. The musician may already have a booking, but they might be willing to change it or have it covered by another musician if the offer is good for them. The important factors are the hours and the budget. I can speak from personal experience about when an agent asked me about my availability for a certain date without any other information. I may have had an afternoon gig but been able to play that night, or I may have had a nighttime gig and been able to play that afternoon, but I didn't know what the agent was offering so I just said I wasn't available. If they had offered me a time and a certain amount of money, I might have been able to make arrangements to do the gig.

Jane tells me that she will ask a musician, "What do you need to make this happen?" She recommends that an artist speak up for themselves and be clear about what they want to do the gig. The first and probably the biggest example of knowing what you want and telling an agent what you want would be your fee. Don't be afraid to tell the agent exactly how much money you want to do a gig.

With a place where she has control of the calendar at 5 locations and she's booking 60 to 70 musicians each month, she can charge the owners 10% or more and never take money from the musicians. In Jane's case, the venue or the promoter pays her to handle booking the music. She also explains that she spent many years having to chase her percentage fee from musicians and it's very time-consuming. She tells me that a well-established agent won't do that anymore. He or she will invoice their clients on a schedule, like once a month. Each agent-client relationship may be different in regard to how they handle their accounting and send out their checks. She thinks it's beneficial to everybody involved to work the system this way and it is how she has done it for a long time now. From my point of view as a working full-time SAM, I like the fact that I don't have to give part of my fee to the agent. It's nice that it's all taken care of behind the scenes between the agency — in this case, Jane — and the venue management or ownership. This process sounds very organized and professional to me.

I ask Jane about her roster and how many musicians she is currently working with. She starts by talking about tribute bands, telling me she has about twenty on her list from all over the country. When I ask about how many SAMs she is working with, she explains to me that she has a list of about fifty solid SAMs she is booking and moves around to different locations of eight venues now. Then there is a layer of peripheral people who fill in and supplement the calendars. Along with those are all the SAMs that are trying to get gigs with Jane, and would be new additions to her roster or calendars.

Jane explains that getting on the roster and becoming a regular part of the rotation has a lot to do with what the venue likes. Her one client has five locations, and she tells me that one nice thing about them is that they send her a weekly e-mail report. After the weekend of music, she is messaged about who they liked and who they didn't like. These managers also share with her the customer reviews that they received, as well as what their employees think. When they do this, Jane can make notes so that she knows which locations like which musicians. This is a behind-the-scenes thing that a Solo Acoustic Musician may not be aware of. It also makes me consider that one location may really like me, and another location's manager may decide I am not a good fit. It's OK, though; as a working SAM, I will not take it personally if I don't fit in at one of the locations and I will just try to do my best each time.

Another thing that Jane can use to gauge how a musician does in a venue is to ask them how they did in tips. She explains that there can be an age difference between servers and customers. If a SAM is playing '70s and '80s music for the customers in front of them, they might be making great tips while younger employees may be wishing for a different musician. Jane is most concerned that the customers are happy. She adds that if you're not hearing anything, everything is probably going well. The meaning here is that people tend to complain more than they praise, so if she's not getting any news at all, then things probably are going well. When things don't go well, she hears about it right away and addresses the situation with the musician.

I will tell you a little story about a gig that I booked with Jane, as an example of how things go wrong sometimes. One of Jane's clients is a golf course, and they have a restaurant with a bar at the clubhouse. They like to have Solo Acoustic Musicians on Friday nights for a three-hour shift. I had played there three times in the past and was loading in one Friday night last winter. They usually like to have music out on the big porch overlooking the golf course, but that night the temperature was in the 40s so I went to find the manager in the office and discussed where I could set up in the bar. The manager wanted me to play outside, but as I live in Florida, 40 degrees is very cold for me. I replied that there were only two gentlemen smoking cigars out on the porch and that everyone else was inside, and that it was too cold for me to be outside.

I could tell he wasn't happy about it, but he relented and showed me a spot to set up in the lounge. One of the other times I had played there in the past I had been told to set up inside, so I thought it was OK and everything would be fine. At the end of the night, I had $111 in my tip can and customers had been giving me praise and telling me that I was good, and I thought things ended well. The next day, when I got on my computer in the morning, I had an e-mail from Jane telling me that the manager did not want me to play there anymore because I had an attitude problem, was hard to work with, and customers had complained about me. So I called her right away to discuss the situation, and told her how I thought the night went and what I thought happened. Jane did ask me how I did in tips, and I told her. So, I know from personal experience that she will ask a SAM this question and it means something.

She has a difficult job as an agent when she is trying to balance so many managers and musician interactions. I can appreciate her taking a few minutes to talk to me on the phone about the gig and ask me what happened that night. Taking the time to get my take on things goes a long way toward building trust and figuring out what happened. I don't like to lose clients at all, but I had to suck it up and move on because that manager decided he didn't like me. Jane handled her job very professionally and I tried to do the same, but it just didn't work out for me at that location, and that's OK; it happens sometimes.

If a musician calls one of the venues that Jane is the agent for, they will be directed to the venue's website to fill out a band booking form. There is a corporate office where all their location's websites are handled. The Marketing Director forwards this information directly to Jane and doesn't spend time evaluating any of the forms.

At her other venues, the musicians will be directed to email Jane. She wants to see links to websites, YouTube, etc. A one-page EPK or website that is direct and can be viewed quickly is what Jane wants to receive in an email. In her opinion, any agent is going to devote about one minute to evaluating the material a musician sends in an email. She is going to listen to the first thirty seconds of a YouTube link or promo video and then scroll ahead a bit to see if the musician is going to show her a variety of musical styles. She doesn't want to hear one whole song. She wants to hear you playing an upbeat song and a slow song, or different genres of music. She even likes to hear some original music, if possible, to get a better sense of the musician's personality. When she really likes something, she will sit and listen to it longer, and may even look at more of their website or information and watch more of their video. Her advice for a Solo Acoustic Musician is to keep their video to about two minutes. She also says to include information in your email or videos like the names of artists and the decades (the '70s, '80s, '90s, '00s, etc.) of the songs you cover. She wants to see that you have a broad range and can be versatile depending on the demographics of the audience in front of you.

One of the best or easiest ways to get a gig through Jane is to have a reference from another musician that she works with and highly respects. She offered a few examples of finding quality musicians because of another musician telling her about them. If the musician already on her roster is really good and easy to work with, communicates well and shows up on time and does a good job, when they suggest another musician for her to check out she will give them a chance. As I wrote in SAM 1 and as was discussed in SAM 2, it sounds like networking with other musicians can also help land gigs booked through agents like Jane.

She wants to know what kind of social media presence they have, and if they have a following, though some venues may not care about that. She does say that the venue likes to know that the musicians are advertising along with them, though. She adds, "Who doesn't want their friends to come to see them play? Or other people who have seen you play before and like you?"

Email is her preference for contact because she can put communications into folders on the computer and even print things out. She uses her computer a lot and although she also uses her phone, she doesn't want it to be the main platform her business depends on. She likes to have information stored in physical paper folders as well, which I believe is important in any business. She tells me she thinks agents who rely too much on their phones make more mistakes, which is how double-booking two musicians on the same gig happens. Jane adds that it is very rare for her to have a double booking at one of her venues. I think she is very organized and communicates clearly with her musicians and venues.

Jane also says that she prefers to talk on the phone rather than texting. Some musicians just want to text her, and she doesn't like that. She would rather hash out a situation quickly with a few minutes on the phone talking. She adds that she doesn't want to get into long conversations, but it is way more efficient to talk instead of waiting for a text reply.

When it comes to managing the calendar, Jane stays booked sixty days out. For example, when we speak she is working on and finishing up November on eight different calendars for her local Solo Acoustic Musicians. It is the beginning of August and before the end of the month, the November dates will be completed. September and October calendars are already fully booked and approved by the venues. This lets me know that by mid-September, Jane will be booking for the December calendars. As I continue working with her, I will receive monthly updates and notifications about turning in open dates to her. Once a calendar is fully booked, she will send out emails for confirmation and then another email with everyone's name, date, time, and location listed for the month. It is important to note that part of my job is to make sure that the dates I booked with her are correct and to only let her know if there is a discrepancy of any kind. Jane also shares with me that one thing about booking too far ahead is that you can lose the opportunity to add new people to the rotation. She says that she knows that some of her regularly booked musicians get frustrated if they get passed over one month, but she must keep current and try new people too. Part of what this is all about is keeping things fresh and entertaining. Most of her core roster musicians are well-established in the area and should be able to stay booked regardless of how many gigs they get from her.

As her work on a month of calendars gets underway, Jane will email and ask SAMs for open dates. Then she will use pencil and paper to make the first draft for each location. She suggests that the SAMs send in dates and make sure, if they are working with a venue or agent in this way, that they state that these dates are open right now. As she explains to me this part of her process, she lets me know that she moves as fast as she can on coordinating and organizing the calendars. She can't hold SAMs hostage over dates. As SAMs, we must be able to fill in our calendars as gigs become available. Constant communication and responding to Jane promptly are necessary. Making sure to confirm dates and times is important.

With the experience Jane has from years of being an agent she knows when things slow down for venues and when people do more traveling. Something that could easily be overlooked, but Jane is fully aware of and handles in a professional manner, is football season. It can have a major influence on fall calendars. Not just the pros, either, because college football is a big deal too. All these things are important in managing all her venues' calendars.

It is a lot of work to handle the number of calendars and shifts that Jane books. Knowing and being prepared for changes is part of her job as an agent. She looks out for the musicians by sending out email reminders about things like changes to the schedule for football season. By doing this she is giving them a heads up that Saturdays at some of her venues will be not booking music for a few months. The musicians who may count on getting a Saturday booking with Jane will now know that they need to aggressively fill in their Saturdays for the time being with different spots. It shows me that she cares about the musicians and is trying to make sure everyone has the information so that they can make good decisions for their calendars.

I ask her why she would continue to put someone on the calendar and why she would stop putting someone on the calendar. Jane tells me one of the things she's very proud of, is having SAMs with good character, not just talent, she wants to be sure she hires people that don't abuse alcohol, which is why none of her musicians get a bar tab as part of their fee. Free sodas, iced tea, water, and coffee are totally part of the deal, as well as at least 50% off of food so the musicians can get a meal on a gig. There are no musicians she books without having a long conversation before the first time, and she tries to get to know them. She feels that she can get a vibe for working with them by having a nice talk.

I ask Jane if she can estimate how many musicians contact her about gigs in a week or a month, just to see... She answers that she gets a ton of voicemails all the time. She says she often gets messages from rappers, a type of music she doesn't work with or hire for her venues based on her client's preferences. She gets messages from people that don't know anything about the music business and think that she is a talent manager for individuals or bands. By this, I mean an exclusive manager to help get them from nowhere to a record deal. She says they probably do an online search and find her company and contact her hoping they can find the help they're looking for, but that they don't really know what an agent does. Then she must explain to them the difference between management and an agent.

A story Jane shares with me that's out of our normal areas of conversation, but that I feel is important to know, is about a musician being involved in a felony domestic abuse charge situation. The guy still lives here and still plays in the area, but five years ago Jane was working with him as well. A couple of other people made her aware of this situation in his personal life and shared with her verifiable proof that it was true. Jane called him and said that she did not want to continue booking him at her venues. She did not want to book him in a venue with a lot of female employees and take the chance of him being inappropriate in any way.

I can respect her decision as well as her professionalism to contact him and explain her stance. It wasn't a rumor, or someone else talking trash about him. As a SAM it's important to behave on a gig, but you have to be mindful of how you act in life as well. You may lose clients based on facts, reputation, hearsay, or any number of other reasons based on your actions outside of a gig. A lot of times, people won't even tell you why they stopped hiring you, so at least Jane did the right thing, in my opinion, by communicating with him why she would not be working with him anymore.

Jane tells me that she feels blessed in all her years of being an agent and that she doesn't have a lot of bad stories to share. There was a musician who blatantly lied to her once. A SAM didn't show up for his gig and told her a really embellished story about what happened. She shared that story with the management at the venue, because she thought it was true and wanted it to be true and she wanted to believe the musician. The manager called B.S. and said the musician was lying.

The venue manager called Jane and said, "Where is our musician tonight?" Jane went into crisis salvage problem-solving mode. When the musician finally talked to her, he said that a friend of his who used to be his roommate took his car without his permission while he was asleep, and he didn't get it back in time, and then he fell asleep again and he didn't want to tell Jane when he woke up because he knew she would be mad. In the meantime, the venue had no musician. This situation affects a lot of people. Maybe the person that writes the checks for the musicians that weekend has written the checks on Tuesday, and they aren't going to be there that night to write a check for a different musician, even if she can get someone to show up last minute to cover the shift. Maybe the bar has advertised on their social media that this performer is going to be there and now he's not. There's a lot going on behind the scenes, and showing up on time or calling the agent and telling them you can't make it to the gig are very important.

Jane tells me that if you're not consistent with her, if you're not honest and transparent, then she can't deal with you. She is always going to tell the truth about anything and everything she possibly can. You will never think Jane is not being transparent with you. She can't operate any other way; it's just who she is. She can cover for musicians if they communicate with her, and she gives me an example from just a week earlier.

A musician on her roster went out to her car and her car was sputtering and making some noise and she didn't know what to do. This is a musician who is 20 years old, who Jane just started working with a few months ago. Jane told her to call an Uber or call a friend and get to the gig. Jane told her, this is your job now and you're calling me an hour before your gig on a Friday which is not good. You need to figure it out and make it happen. If you start a little late, you can skip a break and or play 15 minutes longer. Make up for being late the best you can. But the important thing is right now to get a ride to the gig, play the gig, and get paid, and then the next day get your car to the shop for repairs. Jane told her that she was going to call the venue manager and tell them that the performer was going to be late. This is part of what an agent does behind the scenes and is important — being the liaison between the musician and the venue and trying to keep everything calm and on track.

As we are winding down our conversation, I tell Jane about how I have started keeping track of how many new songs I was learning and that I don't play the same songs or sets every time. She comments that what I'm doing is good, because she hears from managers that tell her the staff is complaining about a Solo Acoustic Musician playing the same songs in the same order every time they are in that venue. She expresses to me that the staff notices and it's not good. I have written about this before and it was nice to hear from an agent that I was correct.

Right before we leave the restaurant, Jane says to me, "Michael, the musician needs to be real with themselves about what they need to work successfully, and the agent needs to be transparent with the artist. You must develop a good working relationship where you trust each other and follow the rules. It's as simple as that." She adds that her rules go beyond what the state of Florida asks on the business side. She offers an example of wardrobe: when she tells a musician not to wear a T-shirt and to make sure they have a collared shirt on for a certain gig, they need to make sure they listen to her. Another example she offers is to not show up at a gig in flip-flops, to make sure they are wearing nice closed shoes. You can't wear a ball cap, but you can wear sunglasses. These were just examples of a few rules for etiquette on a gig. Whatever it is, whatever the rules are that she gives the musicians to follow, there's a reason for it. And if people can't follow those rules, she makes a noise (swoosh) as if she's sweeping somebody off the list and says, "There's a zillion people waiting to get into your space on the roster." At this point in her career and after years of building her business, she can pick and choose which musicians she books. Jane doesn't have to work with anybody that she doesn't want to work with. Working with a SAM who has a bad attitude is not something she is willing to do at this point in her career. She will go out of her way to try to mentor SAMs and give them advice, especially young or new SAMs that aren't very experienced with the gig lifestyle. I think she shared a lot of good advice with me.

On the way home, I am driving through the rainstorm that was generating a lot of thunder while we were talking. It is August and part of our rainy season here in Florida. I continue thinking about all the things we discussed, and feel completely happy with how the interview went. Jane was very open and forthcoming in her answers, and she really shed some light on being an agent as well as what she expects of a Solo Acoustic Musician. It was fun to learn more about her background in the music industry and I am grateful for her sharing her thoughts and wisdom with us. As a musician, I don't get to hang out with the agents very often and I had fun listening to Jane talk about her life as an agent. A nice side effect of this interview is that she and I know each other a little bit more than before, and our working relationship will be even better in the future.

IV. DEAN LAMBERT

Big Top Brewing, Sarasota, FL
2:30 PM – Monday, August 15th, 2022

At the moment I play a gig every Monday evening in Sarasota, Florida. It's over an hour's drive south from my house and I cross the Skyway bridge, which is a Tampa Bay icon, to get there. I left my house an hour and a half earlier today so that I could stop off at the brewery and meet up with Dean. A mutual friend introduced us to each other about two years ago when I was playing a gig somewhere else in Sarasota. He really liked what I was doing and now books me at one of the Big Top locations in Lakewood Ranch, FL, about ten miles north of the original location. I like playing there for a few reasons. The staff is super nice to me, there is a cool stage to play on, and the audiences are always fun. I like to think Dean and I have become friends, so this should be a comfortable and relaxed interview.

A little side note for you that I think is funny: Out of habit, when I arrive, I walk over to check for standing water on the outdoor stage. It has been raining all day and was even lightly raining when I got there, and I wanted to see if the stage is dry. I used to play at the old location, even playing in the rain sometimes. The old stage stayed dry. Here in the new location, less than a mile from the old one and with the same big top circus-style tent roof over the stage, it was only a little wet around the outer edge. It's a big stage that is built to accommodate large bands and it is barely wet a foot in on only two spots of the outer edge. For a SAM like me, it would be completely dry right in the middle of the stage. Later, right before the interview ends, Dean tells me he never cancels for weather except in the case of a tropical storm or a hurricane, where the whole brewery would most likely be closed for the day. Each of the four locations is different and this one has an outdoor stage. I mostly play at another location that has an indoor stage. I like that for myself. I don't have to stress at all because of rain or weather, I am in the air-conditioning, and in the winter, I don't have to worry about being cold.

Dean's history with booking musicians started quite a while ago when he lived in Boston and managed a band. He says it was one band at the time and it was the opposite of what he does now, because he was out trying to get them gigs. He thinks learning from that experience helps him understand the struggle of a Solo Acoustic Musician to keep their calendar full. Dean tells me he was calling venues from Maryland all the way up into the northeast. There are some major markets between DC, Baltimore, Philadelphia, New York, and where they were in Boston. Part of his job was getting the band shows at iconic venues like CBGB in New York and Hammerjacks in Maryland. What he ended up doing for local shows in the Boston area was renting out a club for the night. He would then assemble a bill that included multiple bands. He could book five bands for a night and charge $8 to get into the show. Then he would give each band their cut and the venue would keep the money from the bar sales. Dean would have been considered a concert promoter of sorts.

Dean moved to Florida in August 2009 and became involved with the local music scene in the Sarasota area. In 2010 he bought three franchise locations of a taphouse company that had spread all over Florida and the country at the time. At these three locations, Dean chose to mostly hire Solo Acoustic Musicians with a few duos mixed into the roster. He had three calendars that included Friday and Saturday nights. That would be eight gigs per month per location, for a total of twenty-four spots a month. He tells me that it was usually six SAM spots and two duo spots. The duos were acoustic guitar duos presented in the same way as the solo acts. For special occasions or big events, Dean would hire a band, but the Friday and Saturday night music was focused on SAMs. Even though he was an owner and could have delegated the music program to someone, Dean tells me that it is his passion and he wanted to be hands-on when it came to the music for his three establishments. He owned these venues for about six years.

After that, Dean went to work at another local brewery in Sarasota. There he was also involved in helping with the music program, which was again mostly Solo Acoustic Musicians. He left there after about a year and a half to join the management team of a smokehouse restaurant with a bar that also has a stage for live music acts. The roster was a blend of SAMs and full bands, and Dean was handling all the bookings for the entertainment calendar.

These days Dean is the Regional Director of Operations for Big Top Brewing Company. This title encompasses a lot of responsibilities, including overseeing the entertainment calendars. He is directly responsible for booking the musicians for both Sarasota area locations and is involved with and included in the other two locations' music programs. I have called Dean before and he told me he was in Pensacola at one of the other locations, so I know he goes to the other parts of the company to visit in person. Each location has its own music program. We are at the original location right now as we talk, and it is all bands except for Monday nights, which is always a Solo Acoustic Musician act. The other local location in Lakewood Ranch, just up the road, is almost all SAMs with maybe two bands on the roster. At this location, Dean has also set up an acoustic-based open mic night on Thursdays. The host of the open mic plays every Sunday as a SAM as well. I ask Dean if he ever goes to the open mic in Lakewood Ranch to scout talent. He tells me that pretty much everybody he books there is someone he has seen playing somewhere else. Then he lists several other music venues in the area as examples of where he has seen people play. I believe he goes out looking for good musicians and he likes to hang out and be on the scene. To be honest that's how I met Dean. A mutual friend told him to come to see me play at another establishment, and he showed up with some friends. When I went on break, this friend introduced us with the intention of helping me get a gig at Big Top. It worked out for me, and I am thankful for the reference and introduction. Dean adds that he doesn't think he's ever booked a musical act without seeing them first or knowing of them.

Dean's preference for first contact is email. He tells me that when people at venues used to give out his number, his phone would ring constantly with musicians calling him trying to get a gig. I laugh at this, thinking about his phone just never stopping ringing, and he giggles and says, "You know, it's not my only job here." Dean adds that 90% of the emails he gets contain a video or a link to a video.

When it comes to managing the calendar, Dean tries to be fair and give everyone a shot at playing in the brewery. He tells me that musicians approach him and say they want to be on the calendar once a month, but he only has eight spots at each location. Then he asks me a question: "Michael, in the Sarasota area, like anywhere else, how many Solo Acoustic Musicians do you think there are out there trying to get gigs?" He answers his own question by saying there are probably a thousand and I reply that there are probably more. It's tough with only eight spots to fill, and he already knows a lot of musicians from being a part of this music scene for more than 10 years. Dean even expresses to me that sometimes he feels bad when he has to say no, because everyone is trying to get a gig and most of them are doing it for a living.

I will add here that this probably has a little bit to do with the fact that when he was managing a band, he was the one out there hustling to get a gig booked. So he knows and understands the struggle of musicians. Dean shares with me that there are musicians he knows that don't gig for a living because they have jobs or careers, but they are out looking to play as well. He tries to give some priority or preference to the full-time bands and SAMs. At this point, he gives me a fictional example of a guy in real estate who has four houses listed and just made a $20,000 commission and then comes to the brewery and asks him for a gig... He will feel less guilty about not getting him on the calendar right away. He won't ignore the guy, though, and he'll tell him that maybe he can get him on the calendar once every three or four months. He understands that this guy isn't relying on gigs to pay his bills.

Dean tells me that a local full-time Solo Acoustic Musician reached out to him recently and said, "Hey man, I really need some gigs." This is a person he knows and likes, so he is going to go out of his way to get him on the calendar a little more. I am surprised and interject that this is a perspective I've never heard before. Listening back to the recording, I can hear the surprise in my tone of voice. I tell Dean there are a lot of times where it really seems like us against them with differ-ent venue representatives, and that it's enlightening to hear that he really does care about the musicians.

Sticking with the adage that if you scratch my back, I'll scratch yours, Dean tells me that maybe somebody cancels last minute, and he calls some musicians, and the one that can help him by filling in, he will remember. He says obviously he'll try to do them a favor soon because they did him a favor and helped him out.

His deadline for having the next month fully booked is the 21st of the current month. He is usually done long before that, but that is his personal deadline. Dean says that as of six days from our conversation, he will make sure that all four calendars are completely booked for September. This part of his job includes the Pensacola and Gainesville locations as well, and he does have managers there working on the music program, but he will be in constant contact with them and oversee everything. He even goes so far as to make suggestions about bands or SAMs and steps in if he feels he needs to help get things organized properly. Especially if he sees them getting lazy by doing something like booking the same act every Friday night for two months straight. Of course, it can work, depending on the venue, to have a musician scheduled on Monday, Tuesday, Wednesday, or even Thursday or Sunday in a weekly capacity.

Dean gives me a quick rundown about different venues having different types of clientele based on locations. Things like, do they just need background music to keep people there, are things super touristy so there are different people all the time, or does the place really rely on a lot of regulars too? In the latter case, it probably won't work if you have the same entertainment every Friday night. He gave an example of a conversation that people might have...

"Hey, where do you guys want to go tonight?"

"Well, you know Michael is playing at Big Top."

"Yeah, but you know what, so-and-so is playing over at such-and-such venue."

"Yeah, but we see Michael all the time and he is always there..."

"Let's go to a different place and see someone new or someone we don't see as often."

That's why Dean tries to mix it up as much as possible and keep things fresh. He does book some dates for Solo Acoustic Musicians and some traveling bands where he must plan farther out on the calendar. He knows that some of his favorite SAMs are filling in their calendars a little farther out, so it creates a roster that he balances. His monthly deadline is always in effect.

Big Top does provide a stage and some P.A. speakers for the musicians to use if they want.

When it comes to hiring a musical act, Dean tells me that he goes by a gut feeling. I didn't know this when our conversation began, but both Sarasota locations have an open mic on Thursday evenings. Dean likes to hang out and have a beer after work, so he enjoys the open mic nights. He tells me that if he sees a musician come out a few weeks in a row and play different songs and he enjoys what they're doing, he may approach them about a booking. He says that he has booked quite a few SAMs for Lakewood Ranch because they came to the open mic at the original location in Sarasota. Dean comments that he can tell if they're talented, if they have a good voice, and if they're not playing the same two or three songs every week so that he can get a sense that they are diverse or learning more songs. It's then that he might approach them and ask if they have three hours' worth of material. Dean also says some of the musicians approach him and say, "Hey, I'm coming to the open mic the next few weeks, here's my card. Do me a favor and listen. Tell me what you think." Dean likes to participate in the venue as part of the crowd.

Just the other day I was playing a gig and a couple in the crowd requested a couple of songs. On my break, I went and talked to them a little bit and learned a few of their favorite bands. When I got back up for my next set, I played some of those groups' songs. As they were leaving, they stopped at my merch table to give me a tip that also included a business card with their contact information. That's when they told me that they were owners of another bar and would like to hire me to play. So I'm just telling you that you never know who's in the crowd; a person like Dean could be watching you play and thinking about hiring you.

When it comes to continuing to hire a musician at his venues, Dean says it's super easy for him to decide. He says that for every musician he hires, especially at the two locations in the Sarasota area, he always looks at their personal social media pages or their websites to see what they're doing to help promote themselves. If he sees a big effort, he's happy. He offers the example of a couple of local SAMs who will make a post for every single gig they have, even including a weekly gig post. On the other hand, if he books someone and looks at their social media pages and doesn't see a post and they never mention where they are playing, then in his opinion they are just doing it for the money. They don't care if there are two people there or fifty people, or if no one is there — they just want to get paid. Or they are relying on him to do all the promotions. He names another musician who does very well in the area but then with excitement in his voice he says, "but they do super great when they promote their show on their social media!" Dean says there are some times when it's the day of a gig and he'll go on a musician's social media page and won't see anything so he will call them up and say, "Hey can you put something on your page about where you're playing tonight?" He also says that the musicians can kind of get lazy sometimes and he can see it in the numbers, meaning the number of sales and the amount of money brought in on the night of their gig. There can be a big difference between a normal mediocre night with no help with promotion versus an awesome night with good sales numbers because the musician also helped promote the show. Dean explains that a musician has fans on social media that like their pages. He can't reach those people when he makes a post for the brewery. He can only reach the people that like the brewery pages. So he does expect the Solo Acoustic Musicians as well as his bands to post about their gigs, to hopefully let people know that they are playing there.

There are a couple of other factors why he continues to hire someone. Dean listens to his staff and when they tell him, "Hey, that musician last night was really good, and people liked their music. You should bring them back," he will make notes about what they say. This is especially true for the location where I play, because Dean is at the main location the most and relies on communication with the staff at the Lakewood Ranch location. They have a meeting every week and Dean will ask for their thoughts on the music from the previous weekend. He tells me that if he wasn't there personally to see the audience reaction to the musician, he will look at the numbers. So he might ask the staff, "The numbers are good. How did you like the musician? Do the sales numbers have anything to do with so-and-so playing Friday night?" Dean says the staff will give him an honest answer, and I believe it, because more than likely they don't have an ulterior motive to like any musician more than any other. On top of that most of their wages come from tips, and they want happy customers to buy and drink beer and tip well because they're having fun.

He says sometimes they will tell him they didn't really like the musician who played a certain night and that they picked up on the fact that at some point he started smelling like vodka, so they were pretty sure he was going to his car on breaks and drinking. I laugh at this and say, "What?" Dean affirms, "Oh yeah." It happens, I guess, although I am not used to that because I don't do it. Dean tells me that he considers a musician acting this way to be disrespectful, and I agree.

When I bring up firing someone or not booking them anymore, Dean offers a couple of reasons that he would not put someone on the calendar again. He starts by saying he has fired very few bands and that I could put their names down if I wanted to, which makes me laugh. He tells me about a musician who he is still friends with and sees around town, but he will never book them again. Dean even says that he has told them that, and they are still cool. The main reason for this is that the musician was always late to the gig. Customers would be frustrated or even angry and ask the bartender or management or even ask Dean, "When is the band going to start? You guys posted that the music starts at 7 PM. It's almost 8 PM and he hasn't started yet." He adds that if he hires you to play from 7 to 10, then you need to start somewhere around 7:00 and end somewhere around 10. He offers that if someone starts at 7:15 PM because of a technical difficulty, maybe they could skip a break or play till 10:15 to make up for the time that was lost. He is flexible within reason, but it needs to be realistic, and starting at 8 and ending at 9:30 is not going to cut it. Because that's exactly what he says this musician was doing. Not only were they showing up late consistently, they were also ending early. "By acting like this, the guy was never fulfilling his part of the contract," as Dean put it. (There was no paper contract, but an agreement was made between the musician and the venue.) I have never acted like this in all my years of being a full-time musician, so I don't know if it's the popularity getting to this person's head or why they would think this is okay. Every now and then I hear a story like this, and I wonder what that person is thinking. Dean tells me it's not good for the customer because they are unhappy. It's not good for him or the venue because it makes them look bad. Then he gives me an example of a SAM doing the opposite, and saying that he would always book him because he's one of the classiest acts around. He would sometimes start at 6:59 and play until 10:30 PM without taking a break. If the crowd was into it and the energy was there, then the SAM would just roll with the flow of things and play straight through.

Dean says he likes promptness, and he hates long breaks. If you get the crowd going and then you're off talking to your friends on a break for half an hour between sets, people will probably be leaving. You can lose a ton of your audience that way. He understands that you may see friends you haven't seen in a while, and you want to talk to people, but you must get back to the stage in a reasonable amount of time. He tells me they could set an alarm on their phone that buzzes after 10 minutes so they can end their conversations and get back to work. Adding to that, he says you're getting paid to play music and not hang out near the stage with your friends who you haven't seen in two years. Dean concludes that these are the few things that really make him not want to book a music act again.

Dean says that you should put a little effort into your demo or promo video. There is a big difference between a phone aimed up at you at a bar when you are just playing your gig and something that's edited; maybe you have a friend hold and move the camera around. I agree that this is your sales pitch, and as discussed earlier, even if you must hire someone and spend a few hundred dollars to make a really good promo video to get gigs, it will be worth it. Try to think of it like an investment into yourself and your business. You really want to showcase something good.

Dean doesn't just say this stuff without giving me an example, and he tells me about a local SAM who would just put his phone on the table and play a song and then send that to people to try to get gigs. The guy couldn't understand why he wasn't getting good responses. Dean makes his point very clear when he says, "That musician wouldn't send a video like that if he was trying to get a gig in Key West." He would take time to make a good video. He would play the song three or four times to get a good take. Even if it was just on a phone, he would probably get a friend to help him record a quality video. He would put in the effort and make a really good product. He tells me he has seen promo videos where people walk in front of the musician to go to the bathroom or something. Maybe the musician should have tried another take. He returns to the subject of social media and says that he will look at a musician's personal page and or musician's page and see if they are posting about the gigs that they are playing. He looks to see how many likes and comments they have on their posts. He even goes so far as to look at how many views they have on a video, and when the video was posted. I say to Dean that it seems like his advice is to really put some effort into the video and try to establish some social media presence as best you can.

Then Dean asks me a series of questions. "Why does any bar book a musician to play there? What would be my purpose in having a band or a solo or duo play at any of the Big Top locations? Why would I want live music?"

I reply, "Well, if they're a good musician and it's a nice product because they're good at music then that would be a good thing."

Dean nods his head and makes an "uh-huh" sound. He's clearly waiting for me to go further.

I continue, "If people in the room were happy with what they were doing then that would be a good thing."

Dean takes over and says, "Right. Okay." Then he breaks down the purpose of having a Solo Acoustic Musician every Monday at the Sarasota location where we are sitting. The SAM's sole purpose, and he tells the musician right up front, is to keep the run club here as long as possible. They have a run club that meets there every Monday evening. Dean says, "The only way they make money is if the runners are buying beer and staying." With seventy to eighty members coming to the brewery at the end of their run between 5:30 and 7 PM, he wants the musician to engage them and help them have a good time. He says, "So that's one reason. Whoever's here, keep them here."

Dean explains that if it's a Friday or Saturday, people look to the entertainment schedule to see what's going on that night. They are trying to decide where they want to go and what they want to do. They will go to a certain bar because they like the musician that's scheduled. But if you don't tell anybody you're playing, then they don't know. It's a little bit of both. Whoever is here, keep them here, but also help him bring people to the venue. He is running a business and he is trying to make money. If he is hiring a Solo Acoustic Musician and paying them $200 and there are only ten people at the brewery drinking beer who spend $200 that evening, then he is not making money. Both the venue and the musician have to try to get people in the seats. There is a certain return that he needs to meet to make it a successful event. Now, remember, Dean is also working with bigger bands from the local market as well as regional and national touring acts. During this part of the conversation, he is telling me some big money numbers and big crowd draw numbers that some of the groups bring into the brewery. When a band charges $5000 and brings five hundred people to the show and Dean can sell tickets for the event, it works out great for everyone involved. But remember, just up the road is one of the other locations where he hires mostly Solo Acoustic Musicians, and he thinks it's important for them to try to bring their friends and fans to see them play.

Fairly recently, a Solo Acoustic Musician was done setting up, had done his soundcheck, and was getting ready to start his gig when his phone rang. The musician had tears in his eyes when he came in to tell Dean that he couldn't play tonight. Of course, Dean asked, "Why? What happened?" The SAM had just received word from a family member that his dog had died, and he wasn't going to be able to hold it together and play a show. Dean understood, and the musician packed up and headed home. This all happened just as the gig was about to start, so Dean just canceled music for the night and didn't make calls to try to find somebody to fill in. In all my years I've never heard a story like that before, and I'm glad Dean was compassionate to the musician. Sometimes things are just out of our control and life happens. We have to be flexible and able to go with the flow.

Dean shares another story from one of the other places where he used to be the entertainment manager. Evidently, a musician had completed two sets and was going up to the stage to start their third and final set of the evening but was noticeably drunk. Dean says that he didn't think it was from the bar in the restaurant, and that he believed the musician had a bottle of liquor stashed in their vehicle. The guy started his third set but quickly put the guitar down, started running toward the bathrooms, and then puked right in the middle of the dining room between the stage and the restroom. Mind you, this happened while people were eating dinner and trying to have an enjoyable evening.

In the same venue, Dean suspected one of the musicians was taking something a little stronger than alcohol, although he could never prove it. During the second set, the musician was visibly falling asleep while sitting in a chair on the stage, in front of a packed restaurant and bar. My guess would be he was on hard drugs. Dean says the musician pulled it together and was able to get through the gig, but that some customers were asking him what was going on with that guy. In the end, the musician gave Dean the excuse that he was really tired, he had had a long night the night before, blah blah blah...

Dean tells me that he doesn't have a problem with musicians being persistent when they're trying to get a gig. He thinks persistence means they really believe in themselves, and that's a good thing. He says he doesn't mind musicians who text him constantly, and he includes me on that list because he understands I'm trying to stay on the radar and book some dates. He explains that the one thing he doesn't want is for people to think he's ignoring them, because he's not. The event and music calendars are only part of his job, and he has a lot of responsibilities at the brewery. There are times when he just doesn't have time to respond at that moment. Sometimes he will respond to a musician and say, I'm really busy right now, can you just text me again next week to remind me and we will look at the calendar? (From my perspective, he also has a personal life and deserves family time besides all of his responsibilities at the brewery.)

Dean tells me a quick story about a Solo Acoustic Musician who had reached out to him three times through email. He says the musician then started ripping into him for not giving him a date on the calendar. Dean says, "OK, well now you're definitely not going to play here." He shared some quotes from the email; the guy literally asked him, "What did I do to make you hate me?" Of course, Dean's response was, I don't hate you, I've just been busy and not able to respond to your emails right away, I'm sorry. My advice here is to be patient and not do what that musician did. Have some confidence and don't be insecure. While you are waiting for responses from someone like Dean, you can be calling and emailing more potential clients. I really appreciate the fact that Dean understands musicians being persistent and making their sales calls, texts, or emails. He tells me because the Lakewood Ranch location is mostly Solo Acoustic Musicians, he will get ten to fifteen solicitations from that type of musician every day. There are only eight gigs a month he can put on that location's calendar so he can't say yes to every musician's request for a gig.

Let's do some math here and let's just go on the low end of what he said. Ten musicians contact him every day for seven days in a row — that's seventy. Multiply that by four weeks in a month and we get to two hundred and eighty. That is a lot of emails, text messages, and phone calls. He adds Facebook Messenger and Instagram messages to the list of ways they contact him. In addition, a lot of musicians come to the bar and give the bartender a card or packet about their band and ask for the booking manager. I've gotta tell you, that's a lot of communication to deal with on an ongoing basis. He tells me that he looks at everyone's information and responds to the ones that he thinks would be a good fit. I laugh when he tells me that the ones that are like accordion-and-flute acts aren't really what he's looking for, but he gets those kinds of promotional materials.

As our talk is winding down, Dean tells me about one of his staff members who also works at a local music school. She has helped bring some very young musicians to the brewery and Dean will give them one-hour spots opening up before other scheduled bands. He gives me an example of them doing this on a Friday two hours before I play at the Lakewood Ranch location. To me, that sounds like a cool musical happy hour special event. Dean also works with the music school to do a bigger concert event once a month to showcase the kids' musical talents. Of course, the kids tell all their friends, families, and neighbors to come out for the show, so it becomes quite a fun event for everyone involved. Dean says it can be a four or five-hour event and the kids spend all month putting together and preparing their musical show. I'm really impressed with this and think it's a great way for Big Top Brewing Company to be a musical ambassador in the community.

Sitting down and talking with Dean has been informative, and I've enjoyed hearing his thoughts on booking Solo Acoustic Musicians. I have about twenty minutes to drive downtown to my Monday gig at the marina, and I am thinking back on our talk. I didn't know Dean used to manage bands in Boston and even owned some taphouse franchises here in Florida years ago. He can work with Solo Acoustic Musicians from the local scene up to and including local, regional, and national touring bands. I often wonder how people who oversee the calendars get into handling the booking of the entertainment at venues. It is an interesting part of these conversations that I am having with all of these people who are booking talent. He takes the job of putting talent in the brewery and all its locations seriously and handles his business. I hope you picked up a few tips from our talk and can apply them to your journey as a Solo Acoustic Musician.

V. STEPHANIE ANDERSON

Video Phone Call from Tampa, FL to Tacoma, WA

12:30 PM - Wednesday, September 21st, 2022

I had been looking forward to talking to Stephanie for a little while, but we had to reschedule a couple of times because of life. She is a wife and mother, and has a family to tend to as well. I picked up a last-minute gig on another one of our scheduled times to talk. With the time zone difference came the obstacle of timing our interview with our schedules. As they say, the third time is a charm and we were able to use a social media app to video chat.

I don't remember the first time I met Stephanie in person, but I know I first learned about her on Myspace in 2008. I was getting ready to move to Florida from Maryland and was using social media to research venues and musicians in the Tampa Bay area. I was able to visit a few times in the winter before I moved, but when I was back home in Maryland, I found it useful to find venues to approach. It also allowed me to see and hear some of the other musicians in the area. Stephanie was one of the musicians I discovered, and she was working her Solo Acoustic Musician gigs steadily with a full calendar. Seeing this gave me hope and helped me be confident that there was plenty of work and places to play music gigs for money.

Speaking of getting gigs, let's see what she has to say about hiring SAMs for her venues. The title that I give Stephanie is that of the third-party agent. Stephanie has an LLC for her

SAM business, and she operates the agent side under the same company credentials.

Stephanie says she was late learning guitar and started taking lessons when she was in college. She was twenty years old when she started, and has been playing for twenty-six years. After she finished college, she moved to Florida and got a job. She also started going to open mics in the area. She was meeting people in the music community at these events and ended up finding a duo partner. A friend of a friend was looking for someone to play music with, and he is even the one who helped her get into the venue she is still working with today.

Currently, Stephanie is managing the calendars for five locations of a popular seafood restaurant chain in the beach towns near Tampa Bay. She has four locations in Clearwater Beach, and one in Treasure Island. She tells me that she has been managing the music calendars and working with this company for about fifteen years. She says it started out in a casual way. She was playing at one of the locations every Thursday and Saturday. At the same time, one of her friends was playing there every Friday. When either of them needed to cover a shift, she would just handle the calendar and make it happen. She explains that it wasn't official, and they weren't paying her to do it, but if one of them needed a shift covered then she would just find a musician to play in their place.

The transition happened when the restaurant opened another location and the general manager asked her to come in and talk about playing there. That's when he said to Stephanie, "You know a lot of other musicians around here. Would you like to do the booking? I will pay you extra every time you play here." She agreed to manage the calendars for both locations. So after playing there for a couple of years, it became official and she was now the venue representative. As they opened new locations, she would manage the calendars for them as well. When she was about to move to Washington state, she had a conversation with ownership about continuing to manage the calendars remotely and that has worked out for everyone involved. The phone calls, texts, and emails are the same and she doesn't have to be on-site to book the calendars. They were comfortable with keeping her on and not making any changes. When I asked her how long ago she had moved to Washington, she told me it had been about six years and I was actually surprised. I said, "Wow! Has it really been that long?"

It makes sense to me that she would handle venue calendars. As a Solo Acoustic Musician, she is already involved in booking her calendar and networking with other SAMs, so it is a natural extension of her career. It can also help add some stability to her life by being able to book herself into venues where she controls the calendar. In my mind, it's a no-brainer and a smart move.

All of the locations that Stephanie books fall under the category of beach-style restaurant bars. There is a focus on seafood and every one of them is in a tourist-driven beach town. The same company has a few other locations on the east coast of Florida, but Stephanie doesn't handle those calendars. She tells me that she doesn't know any of the musicians over there and wouldn't want to manage the booking for them.

Each time the company has opened a new location here along the beach in Tampa Bay, they have handed her the job of booking the entertainment. There was one exception where another local agent was booking for a venue and when it closed, he convinced the new owners to keep him on to do the booking. Part of the convincing was done by the managers of the previous venue, whom the new owners decided to keep on also. The new owners were the people who own the businesses Stephanie works with. They closed the property down to do some renovations and reopened under their company name.

After a while, it didn't work out with the original agent and eventually, Stephanie took over the responsibility of running this new location's calendar as well.

She shared with me that the other agent in this story had previously approached the owners of her venues and tried to take over the booking. Her bosses told him they were happy with her and declined to work with him. When she moved to Washington, this other agent was also using musicians to try to get the management of her venues to switch. Stephanie was booking dates at her venues with a few musicians who this other agent was also booking, and these musicians were more loyal to him. They were actively bad-mouthing Stephanie behind her back and trying to help the other agent take over her venues. I had never heard of another agent doing something like this and it lets me know just how competitive it is out there in the agency world. Stephanie defended her turf in a professional manner, and was also blessed to have the support and loyalty of the owners of her venues. She does a good job and they were happy to continue working with her as their entertainment director or venue representative. (As an aside, I already didn't like the agent who did this because of his shady dealings in the past, and this story is just another in a long line of confirmations that he is bad news.)

With five locations that offer music seven days a week, Stephanie is working with a core of ten Solo Acoustic Musicians and has a list of more than ten other preferred

SAMs who fill in the blank spots on the calendar. She also tries out new SAMs in the extra spots and communicates with management to see who they like. She explains to me that one small drawback of booking remotely is that she can't go out and see other SAMs from the area live at a gig somewhere else. She says, "People can send you a video and they sound really great in the video. But comparing one demo video to a four-hour live show can be a lot different." She adds that sometimes she will book someone based on their demo video and receive negative feedback from management, but for the most part, the videos do represent the skills and talent level of the musician and she can tell who is on par with what the venue expects. She also relies on referrals or opinions of the Solo Acoustic Musicians she knows and trusts. She will check out anyone her core SAMs recommend and those musicians will get a shot at a date on the calendar. She respects her regulars and thinks that they know what good music is, so she finds it helpful if they send another good musician her way.

Stephanie's roster is mainly made up of Solo Acoustic Musicians. She does have a few steel drum players on her team who focus on Caribbean music. At one specific location, they wanted to have that kind of music added to the mix, especially on the weekends with a focus on reggae, calypso, and island vibes. She confides to me that some of the SAMs use looping station pedals, but her venues have made a distinction between that and using backing tracks. They do not like backing tracks and don't want her to hire musicians who use them. Her venues prefer a live Solo Acoustic Musician act without pre-made backing tracks. Stephanie also has the occasional duo booked on her calendar.

At times Stephanie will be setting up or already playing a gig and get a call from one of her musicians who is canceling.

She will send out as many texts as she can to try to find a fill-in for that shift at that venue. She will keep an eye on her phone and if she can send another text in between songs then she will respond quickly. She handles it the best she can, but obviously, she has her own obligations as well. When she is on a gig, she has to play. She says that she will also text the manager of the venue and let them know that she is on a gig somewhere else and is trying to sort out a fill-in because of someone else canceling, and will do her best to make it work. She says that they are always understanding about the situation and that they knew it would be a possibility because she is gigging as well. She just rolls with it and does what she can.

Stephanie tells me that she gets at minimum a few emails a month from new musicians trying to get a gig. It can be a lot more, and they seem to come in all at once sometimes. When a SAM stops into one of her venues, the managers will give that person her email address as their booking contact. She prefers that they give out her email rather than her phone number, especially with a new person. Sometimes the musicians look her up on social media and she will get personal messages there as well.

When she is checking out a new musician, she focuses on the music, and says that is the main thing she considers when she makes a new hire. She adds that vocals are very important to her and that someone can be an amazing guitar player but if their vocals aren't up to par then she might not hire them. She doesn't think most people in the audience want to watch someone shred on a guitar all night and then not sing well. I agree with her and will share with you that I don't like it when I go to see live music and I can't hear or understand the vocals.

Stephanie also considers what she thinks management and staff are going to think about the sound and type of music.

Her example is that she loves blues, and knows some really good blues players and bands. But the staff in her venues are not into blues music very much and it doesn't seem to work in her locations. She has tried it out more than once, and she told me about a musician she booked at one of her locations. The music is solid and the musician is a good player, but they play specifically blues and jazz and while they were good, the staff didn't really go for it. Part of Stephanie's balancing act is trying to think of what the management, staff, and audience will enjoy while they are spending time in each location. Her venues do like a variety and expect the SAMs to include a blend of classic older songs with newer current music. Happy, beachy styles of music work best because of the locations of all her venues.

After a Solo Acoustic Musician makes it into her rotation, there are things they can do to keep getting booked in her venues. Stephanie values people who are reliable and does not want to work with musicians who flake out on her all the time. She can be very understanding and try to work with people when things come up and they need to cancel a gig. But if somebody is continually disappearing, she can't keep putting them on the schedule.

Beyond constantly having to cancel or reschedule, she has other reasons why a musician might not work out. She is in steady contact with the management of each location to evaluate how the SAMs are doing and relies on their feedback immensely to make decisions about who to keep on the roster. This information goes both ways, because they might like one musician and not like another and they let her know who they want to play there more often. She even tells me that sometimes she personally knows a SAM and likes their music and them as a person but for some reason, the management doesn't think they are a good fit and she has to take them off the calendar. She added that unfortunately at the end of the day, she has to do what management wants.

Being on time for a scheduled performance at one of Stephanie's venues is important to her. Management and Stephanie agree on this, but allow some leeway because of the touristy beach locations. When it is the height of the season in these beach towns, the traffic on and off the islands can be massive. Finding parking can be an issue as well, and they know that musicians may have to start late. In my mind, if they have established a working relationship with a SAM and they are usually on time then when something like this happens, they will understand that abnormal circumstances come up. Management can be flexible and also, they might be so busy they won't be concerned with the musician starting late at all.

Stephanie believes that if you start twenty or thirty minutes late, you should add that amount of time to the end of your gig and play for the full three or four hours that you are booked to perform. We also discussed how that might not be possible if the musician has another gig to go to that day, or if another musician is scheduled in the same location right after the first musician is done playing the afternoon shift. It is easy to make up some time by starting a little earlier the next time at the venue. As hectic as the season is on the beach, there is still a bit of a laid-back attitude, and the managers are cool with the musicians on this matter. She remarked that she has been blessed with Solo Acoustic Musicians who are punctual and that she hasn't had any managers contact her to say that one of them was late all the time. I think it just happens sometimes and everyone just deals with it and moves on.

I asked Stephanie to tell me about things that SAMs do that annoy her and this is what she had to say. She tells me that she appreciates it when people are honest with her. She doesn't want to be lied to about a gig, especially since she is a musician too. She gets it; maybe you just played ten days straight in a row and you are exhausted. She would prefer you say that and ask her to cover your gig rather than lie to her about the situation. She has had to deal with some musicians lying to her in a way that affects the business. One SAM, whom she doesn't work with anymore, flaked out on her too many times. Evidently, he would use his dog as an excuse. Examples of things he would say are... "My dog got out" or "My dog ate a bunch of chocolate and I have to take him to the vet." He even used the "I'm sick with the flu" excuse and then literally the next day she saw him advertising on social media where he was playing that night. The lie also had an effect on the business because that SAM was at one of the other locations the night before he canceled. At that location, a bartender called out sick with a sore throat, and management was worried about a flu bug spreading through the staff. Stephanie had to tell the manager about the SAM who called out sick with the flu, and I think you can see how this "little lie" grew out of control with unforeseen consequences.

He gave her excuse after excuse after excuse until he excused himself right out of getting gigs through Stephanie. She tells me that he recently reached out to her on social media, trying to get back in her good graces. Stephanie points out that he did not apologize for his previous mistakes, and even though it has been more than a year she did not even respond to his message. I have to agree with her on this one, because that SAM was not professional on many levels.

She has also had musicians flake out and just not show up for a shift. She also deals with last-minute cancellations, and she understands that emergencies can happen but she wants to have as much notice as possible so that she can find a replacement. One time a musician texted her that he needed to cancel because of a family emergency. Obviously, Stephanie thought it was something serious and replied to him by saying, "No problem. I will get the shift covered." She was frantically reaching out to other SAMs because it was so last minute. The next day, she reached out to the musician who canceled to ask him how he was doing. He told her that his "family emergency" was that he had stayed out drinking the night before and his wife was mad at him, so he needed the day off to try to smooth things over with her. Stephanie said to me, "That's not a family emergency," and I agree with her on that one too, and laugh very hard, because that cancellation excuse story is ridiculous. Stephanie was stressed out while trying to find a replacement and genuinely worried about the guy and his family. Meanwhile, he was just hung over and his wife was rightfully upset with him over his behavior. She tells me that she likes working with him, that he is usually very professional and he has always been reliable in the past. But even the good ones have a hiccup once in a while and make bad decisions.

When it comes to finding a replacement to cover a shift, Stephanie prefers to find a musician herself. She does not want the SAM who is canceling to just send another musician in their place. She has her list of approved SAMs to call when this situation arises. She particularly doesn't want them to find a replacement that management has already told her not to book anymore. She does trust most of her musicians and if one of them said they needed to cancel but they have found a replacement, she has the authority to approve that but wants the heads-up and for them to communicate with her. Of course, it would make things easier for her if the SAM provided another SAM to cover their shift.

One SAM did not abide by this rule and I am going to try to explain the situation that Stephanie had to deal with because of this person's actions. A SAM who was playing a steady Monday gig at one of her locations was also taking gigs around town from the other agent who was trying to take over her venues. The guy was in league with the other agent on some level and was trying to help him undermine Stephanie. He was having other SAMs cover his shifts without consulting her. Management and bartenders started to tell Stephanie that the guy hadn't shown up and had sent some other random SAM that they didn't know in his place. Evidently, they didn't like the replacement. Stephanie had no idea that this was happening and evidently, it had happened several times before she was told about the situation. Stephanie tells me that she had discussed her policy with this Solo Acoustic Musician. She conveyed to him that if he needed to cover a shift then he needed to let her know so that she could communicate that information with management. She also explained that she had to approve whoever was going to be the replacement SAM that is covering the shift. But the guy just kept sending other people to cover his Monday shift without telling her. Needless to say, Stephanie has a good relationship with the owners and management of her venues and was able to explain what was happening and make moves to fix the problem. That SAM doesn't play there anymore.

Stephanie has her core SAMs locked into spots on the weekdays. The same person every Monday and so on through Thursday. These spots are filled in advance for each location. The rest of the calendar dates are only booked a month or two in advance. Most of the shifts are four-hour gigs, with the exception of one location where the shifts are three hours. The four-hour shifts will run from 5 to 9 PM or 6 to 10

PM. All five locations have music seven days a week. At two of the locations, she can have two shifts on Saturdays and Sundays, based on the time of year or the season: 1 to 5 PM in the afternoon and 6 to 10 PM in the evening. One location has a 12 to 4 PM Saturday afternoon shift and no evening shift. Along with their paycheck, each location offers a $25 tab for the musician's food or drinks. After she sends in a monthly invoice, the main office pays Stephanie to run all five calendars and she does not charge the musicians a fee of any kind.

Stephanie runs a tight ship when it comes to managing her calendars and double bookings do not happen very often. Out of all these years, it has only happened a couple of times. When it's Stephanie's fault, she will make sure to give the SAM some extra gigs to make up for the mistake. One time she even paid the SAM for the gig because she felt so bad and because it doesn't happen very often. She tells me that one thing that happens every now and then is a mix-up over which location the SAM is supposed to be playing. With five locations that all have the same name, four of them in the same beach town, a SAM can show up at the wrong spot. So when two SAMs are loading in at the same time, they can take a minute to communicate with her and get things squared away.

Out of all five locations that she books, only one is completely weather permitting. The other four are inside or have an alternate stage area in case of bad weather. Stephanie makes sure that the SAMs know this before they agree to take a gig in that specific venue.

When new SAMs are reaching out to Stephanie, she likes them to include all the important information in their first email. She tells me that some people will take ten emails to convey what should have been in one. A lot of unnecessary back-and-forths can be eliminated, and communication can be quick and clear. She also dislikes when musicians are in essence harassing her. She understands that you need to follow up with venue representatives and be on top of your business when you are trying to get gigs, but don't call or email them every day. Stephanie doesn't want to hurt anyone's feelings and she tries to be nice to all the musicians who approach her for gigs. Sometimes she just doesn't like their music and she doesn't want to make them feel bad or diminish their hopes and dreams in any way, so she might just tell them that her calendar is fully booked and she will keep them in mind for fill-ins. Remember that she has multiple venue management teams that she works with, and she might not think the SAM is a good fit musically for what they want.

She tells me that one SAM is being overly persistent with her, to the point of rudeness. He is emailing her constantly and saying things like, "Hey, aren't you tired of the same old same old at your venues? Aren't you ready for someone new?" She has told him repeatedly that she doesn't have anything for him at this time, but she will keep him in mind if she has any last-minute cancellations. She is trying to be kind, and when she is describing this situation to me I can tell by her tone of voice that this person has emailed her way too much and way too aggressively.

She tells me that another SAM emailed her to say that he went to one of her venues the other night and the Solo Acoustic Musician was horrible, and that she should book him instead. She says to me, "Don't do that." She explains that these two SAMs are now harassing her, and it's not helpful and makes her not want to give them gigs or work with them. She responded in a professional way and didn't ignore them and now it is too much on their end. I offered my thoughts about what she told me. On a deeper level, this musician had just insulted her by saying the other SAM she hired wasn't good. I don't know if musicians realize that when they are putting down another musician, they are also putting down the venue representative that hired them. By saying what he said, he has also disrespected Stephanie's judgment, and that is the opposite of what he should be doing when trying to gain someone's favor. In my opinion, you are not going to convince someone to book you in their venue by putting down the other musicians that they hire. I am pretty sure that this particular musician is probably never going to be working with Stephanie.

After we talk for about an hour, I stop recording, and we catch up a little bit more, sharing about our personal lives. I learn more about how much work she puts into running the calendars for her venues while balancing her own musical gig schedule and family time. I hope you can pick up some good advice from what Stephanie shared. She is familiar with both what we do and what the person hiring you is looking for when you are trying to get a gig. It's a unique and rare perspective to have, because she is a full-time working Solo Acoustic Musician who also manages five venue calendars, booking SAMs seven days a week.

VI. TARA HAGAR

Cotee River Brewing Company, New Port Richey, FL
4:45 PM - Wednesday, October 12th, 2022

The town of New Port Richey, FL is about a thirty-minute drive north of my house normally, without heavy traffic, but sometimes it can take forty-five minutes or even up to an hour to get there in Friday rush hour traffic during tourist season. It's always a little shorter ride home at the end of a gig. Today, I am going there on a Wednesday to talk with Tara and hopefully Bryan as well. I have been playing music at this brewery for a few years now and really enjoy my time there. I have become friends with the team and they are my place on Main Street in this town. Thanks to the mutual respect and loyalty we have built, though we have no exclusivity agreement, I don't play the other music venues in the downtown area.

I have never been sure of Tara's title, so we start there; she tells me she is the brewer's assistant. She also has other responsibilities that she admits haven't ever really been labeled. She is a bartender. She handles booking the live music. She also books the food truck slots on the calendar. I think of her as a general manager who wears several hats in the brewery. Under the umbrella of management, I would add these titles to her resume:

General Manager - Brewer's Assistant / Bartender / Entertainment Director / Food Truck Liason / Social Media Supervisor / Local Craft Beer Ambassador

She has a lot going on in the brewery and puts in a lot of hours there. I include the title of Local Craft Beer Ambassador because Tara goes out to other breweries and connects with customers, employees, and owners. She is part of a brewery community that even extends out of her town. Although it may seem that she is just enjoying some beers with friends, she is also representing her brewery and developing contacts. I went with her to St. Petersburg once to check out a handful of breweries down there, and along the way, she was establishing contacts and making connections while at the same time learning about their operations. From helping make the beer to scheduling events and being on-site every day tending to customers, Tara is constantly working on improving Cotee River Brewing.

Her responsibility for the music program started more than a year ago when she took over the calendar from the owner. The Entertainment Director position kind of fell into her lap and she stepped up right away to do the job. The owner was handling the booking for a long time, with the help of another employee who is no longer working in the brewery.

The current musical roster at Cotee consists of eleven recurring acts and a handful of fill-ins. Right now, she books five acts once a month and six that she gives a date to every other month. The majority of these are Solo Acoustic Musicians, though she does hire a couple of duos and two trios. There is an eclectic range of musicians on the roster. One of the trios is a Celtic band, and one of the solo acts they hire is a violinist who plays along with tracks, and most are cover artists playing other people's songs, with the majority playing acoustic guitars.

When I ask Tara about a point of contact for booking a gig at Cotee River, she explains that she prefers musicians to initiate a conversation via a social media message. She tells me that people seem to call when they are closed and leave voicemails and she finds the social media messages easier to manage. She adds that people also like to stop in right when they are opening, and that is a very busy time because of all the setup that is going on to get the brewery ready for the day. She likes that the SAM can send her a video or link via social media. If she doesn't already know who they are, this is an easy way for her to check out their music.

If you message the brewery and ask, "Who do I talk to about your music booking?" she will typically reply with her name and tell you how far out she is booked at the moment, then request a video of some kind. She will follow up by looking at the person's profile page and investigating what they have been up to, seeing what she can learn about them and their music from there. As far as having a preference between a website or a social media page, it doesn't matter to her. She just wants to be able to get information about your music, so the format is not as important as the content. She isn't requiring anyone to audition, but they have been encouraging musicians to come to their open mic if they would like to showcase a few songs in hopes of landing a gig.

Tara says the volume of SAMs requesting to play at the brewery varies; she might receive five to ten messages in one week and none the next week, followed by a wave of messages again the week after that. It seems that on average she has about ten to twenty new Solo Acoustic Musicians reach out to her every month. She also tells me that sometimes they are not even from the local area; they are traveling through looking for gigs. In general, this doesn't work for her because, as she says, "They want to book a gig for the next month, and we are already booked."

When Tara took over as the Entertainment Director, the roster was already developed and she was able to book a whole year out on the calendar with a solid core of musicians that they enjoy hearing. After getting her key people on the calendar she was able to expand the roster and try to fill in spots with a few new SAMs.

While they don't expect the musicians they hire to bring a following, they hope that they will at least keep people who are there happy and entertained. Tara explained that there were a couple of SAMs who weren't doing that, so they don't play at the brewery anymore.

One specific Solo Acoustic Musician was taken off the schedule for a few reasons, and it started with showing up late but evidently, there were also other areas where this SAM was deficient. His tardiness became a habit and was not an isolated event. He was not apologetic or remorseful for being late, either. According to Tara, his whole persona and attitude were of someone who did not even want to be there. He added to the negative pattern he had established by taking a super long break and stopping his show ten minutes earlier than scheduled. Tara says, "At that point, I don't feel he is adding value anymore because he visibly looks unhappy and like he doesn't want to be there. He shows up late and leaves early. So, what is he bringing to the table? It's not a good vibe for the customers." This musician was on the stage projecting a mopey, depressed, yucky aura onto everyone in the room. She says, "Yeah, it's not a good time." As I stated, this was not an isolated event and she did give him multiple chances, but the abysmal scenario persisted so she had to make a change to her roster and the calendar.

Tara tells me that she is fairly forgiving if a SAM is a few minutes late, because the parking situation downtown can be a challenge. She says, "I get it. You can plan to leave your house and arrive at the brewery at the same time every time and then one time you just don't get there on time." But this was a consistent issue that lasted for six months before she decided to take action and let him go from the team. She gave him plenty of chances to rectify the situation, correct the issues and keep his spot on the stage.

As we talked, it occurred to me that I knew who she was talking about and we discussed this individual in a little more detail, off the record. It is unfortunate that things turn out like this sometimes, but that's a part of life and she has to make decisions based on what is good for the business moving forward. Clearly, she made a good decision for the brewery and found another Solo Acoustic Musician who would like to play there and filled in the spots on the calendar easily.

We both chuckle when I ask her what Solo Acoustic Musicians do that annoys her. With a heavy sigh, she tells me how one SAM in particular needed to cancel, and again she is forgiving about things like this because as she says, "Stuff comes up." But this guy contacted the brewery through one of their social media pages and the message was never delivered, so the brewery never responded. He called and left a message while the brewery was closed, and once again nobody responded to him. He never called while they were open to make sure that they had received the messages. The end result was that the SAM just didn't show up for the gig. The brewery didn't have a musician scheduled as backup and he didn't offer to find someone to cover the shift for him, so there was no live music that night. By the time Tara was figuring out what was happening, it was showtime on a weekend night with a taproom full of customers. Cotee River has a consistent schedule of music on Friday and Saturday nights so there were some customers asking about what happened. Tara was frustrated because she didn't really have an answer other than, the musician isn't here and I don't know why. As she puts it, "He didn't make a real effort to communicate what was going on." I asked her how she found out what had happened and she explained that she messaged the guy and asked if he was coming in to play. He told her that he had sent a message and she countered by informing him that she had not received any messages.

I have to interject here and tell you that when I am booking or canceling a gig, I want confirmation. I want to be able to know that I am confirmed either way. I want to be sure that the venue and I are on the same page at all times, and that everyone involved knows what's going on. If I were to reach out to the venue by phone, email, or text and not receive a reply, I would try again and make sure that someone from the venue knew I wasn't going to be there and why.

This SAM never followed up and just assumed that they knew he wasn't coming in to perform. Now he has reached out a few times to book more dates with Tara, but she hasn't hired him again. According to her, that was his first booking with the brewery and her first time hiring him to play there, and as you can tell it didn't go so well. The way I see it, he got his foot in the door, he got a date on the calendar, and then he flaked. I can understand her reluctance to book another date on the calendar with him.

A similar situation just happened last weekend; a Solo Acoustic Musician didn't show up for his shift and when she contacted him, she was told that he was going to be there the next week. Here's the funny part about this. I play here the first Friday of every month and that would have been my shift, so I had to smile because I knew the other musician had definitely made the mistake on his calendar. I have had my spot with Cotee River for a couple of years and Tara would not have made a mistake or miscommunicated about any of the first Friday dates, because they aren't open. She looked at her phone to see, on the same page, a stream of messages where the correct date was confirmed by both her and the SAM. Now I can really see why she was annoyed with this particular miscommunication.

Since we were talking about someone not showing up or wanting to cancel, I asked Tara how she likes to handle the situation. She has her list of SAMs that she can reach out to first. If the musician can offer her a replacement that she has already hired in the past it could be okay. She does not want some random person that she has never heard to be sent in to cover a gig.

I ask her about the promotion of the music events at Cotee River. At the brewery, they don't always post all their events on multiple social media sites. Since they have more things on their calendar than just music, she tries to balance what is there so it's not an overwhelming flood of information for the customers to scroll through. They do, however, make an event for every musician, food truck, etc. and those are all listed, so everything is available for people to see. I get this approach. There is a difference between posting news on a timeline and making an event. They might be posting about bike week and a new fall beer on tap, which is a huge event coupled with a product rollout, so they won't want to clutter up the feed with a couple of posts about which musician is playing that weekend.

In the downtown area where Cotee River is located, there is quite a bit of foot traffic. Being surrounded by other local businesses which include restaurants, bars, and shops makes for a busy town center. Tara has an up-to-date current weekly or bi-weekly list of upcoming entertainment. It's a chalk marker board in the front window so that people walking by can see what's going on in the brewery. It is an old-school way of advertising, but it works — she tells me that she sees people stopping to read the sign all the time.

Tara has decided to change a few things about her process of managing the calendar for the coming year. She booked the whole year of 2022 all at once and well in advance. This year, she is looking at the calendar differently. Because of having to let a couple of people go midway through the year and because she had already booked them farther out through the end of the year, she is only going to commit to the first six months of 2023 at this time. This will give her a chance to hire some new people if things aren't working out with one of the other musicians. By the time April 2023 rolls around, she will know who she wants to keep on the roster and start looking at booking the second half of the year.

She is the only one who has access to the physical calendar book, and is responsible and accountable for all the music bookings on the calendar. If anyone has a question about the music program, they get referred to Tara. This way there is no confusion or double bookings. In her two years of working at Cotee River, she has only experienced one double booking. It happened before she took over as Entertainment Director. One of the bartenders, who is no longer with the company, was dabbling in helping the owner with booking the calendar. This situation led to a mistake.

Tara was behind the bar and serving the customers when a second musician walked into the brewery. There was already a musician set up on the stage and she admits that she didn't know what was happening. She wasn't yet handling the calendar and she didn't have it or know where it was at the time. The musician who was set up already was a regularly hired person who she knew, and the guy who had just arrived was somebody that she had never met before. The second guy had a beer and left, and the first musician played the gig. According to Tara, the new guy was booked through a social media message but not added to the official calendar of events. A situation like this cannot happen anymore, because only one person can book the musicians at the brewery. After Tara took over, she gave the other SAM who went home that day some dates throughout the year, but she says it didn't work out and he no longer plays in the brewery.

As we established earlier, she has five regular monthly acts and there are usually eight total shifts a month. The other six acts that play here once every other month fill the three remaining spots each month. There can also be the occasional fifth Friday or Saturday and even the odd fifth weekend. These are the spots where Tara will book new Solo Acoustic Musicians who are trying to get a gig — she will try out a new person on a fifth Friday and see how they fit in the venue. These dates might also be filled by people that they just don't book on a regular basis.

Here at Cotee River, the Solo Acoustic Musicians are booked for three hours. They have always had live music from 7 to 10 PM on Friday and Saturday nights but have also tried Sunday afternoons. Right now, they are not booking the Sunday shifts because business was not consistent. If that changes, they may bring back that spot on the calendar. Also it is football season right now and people want the sound on for the Tampa Bay Buccaneers games.

Tara tells me that some SAMs like to provide their own break music but most of the time they just turn on the house system when a musician leaves the stage.

I ask her if she gets feedback about the musicians from customers, and she tells me she wishes they would talk to her more about the musicians and the food trucks, especially when they hire new Solo Acoustic Musicians. When she is busy behind the bar serving customers, the music becomes background noise because she is concentrating on bartending. She likes it when her regular customers who are paying attention to the music let her know what they do and don't like. While she is taking orders, ringing up tabs, and pouring beers on a busy Friday night, she can be really hustling around the room, and she won't have time to concentrate on watching the musician. Meanwhile, a customer sitting on a barstool drinking a beer can pay close attention if they choose. She tells me that every now and then a customer will tell her that they don't really like a musician. She says to them, "That's fine. That's your opinion. But we have success with this person and we are not going to change anything." She explains that customer feedback is important, but it's not the biggest factor in making a decision about any particular musician she hires.

I ask her if I was one of the musicians that someone didn't like and she says yes, my name had come up twice. I laugh and ask her, "What did they say?" She tells me that one guy said that I said the "F" word too many times. (In this venue I am allowed and even encouraged to play some of my adult content songs. So I do sometimes.) She remarks that on the day in question, she hadn't heard me say any bad words at all, and she told him that she and the owner were not going to do anything about it. From my perspective, it is nice that the management and ownership had my back, especially since they encourage me to do some of those songs. I laugh and ask, "Who is this guy? A librarian?"

The other time someone expressed their dislike for my music they told her that they just didn't really like what I was doing. Tara's response to this customer was that not every musician is for everybody. I am happy that she defended me; I know not everybody likes me all the time or likes everything that I do, but I also know that a lot of people in that room do like what I am doing, so I can handle the criticism. She added that this customer has complained about multiple things and other musicians, so she just chalks it up to them being unhappy no matter what.

I ask her, "What about other musicians besides me?" She tells me that most of the time the main complaint, if she gets one, is that the music is too loud. The customer will say something like, "We can't talk. It's too loud." Tara comes right back to them and says, "Well I can hear you just fine when I am taking your order and when I'm talking to you right now." You gotta love the spunk. Tara's tough in a good way. She admits that there have been SAMs that she has had to ask to turn down, so she does understand what's going on in the room.

I ask Tara for some advice for a Solo Acoustic Musician from her point of view. Right away she tells me that she is dealing with a situation involving a couple of the SAMs that she books to play at the brewery. Her advice is to not over-saturate yourself in one area. She explains that one of her Solo Acoustic Musicians plays at least four places downtown every month. She says that even if you have a following, they are probably not all going to go see you play once a week at four different locations. She creates a hypothetical example by saying, "What if you have twenty people that follow you?

Now you have given each location an average of five if they split up evenly."

She adds that she doesn't require exclusivity and never asks any SAMs to only play her venue. But she does suggest that they find other parts of town outside of the downtown area to find gigs. Her reasoning is that if you have friends and fans that come see you play, they won't want to go downtown every time. She adds that part of the value of having a musician is if they can bring some friends to hear them play. I want to make a note here that she doesn't require any musician or band to have a following, but it does make sense that that does add value from the venue's perspective. She says one of the SAMs she hires does have a small following, but it doesn't benefit the musician or the venue if they're splitting it up between four different venues in the small downtown center. She also mentions that they have two small bands who have an exclusive deal with them and don't play anywhere else downtown. They have a following and they only play in this venue. I will also add on my own that I only play at Cotee River Brewing in New Port Richey, although I don't have any exclusivity agreement with them either. That's just how I do things and I believe I talked about that in SAM 1.

She also tells me timing is important. I will add that in a way it's kind of like luck. She tells me that she books big blocks of the year all at once and she has several regular musicians she's been working with who get dates before anyone else, which leaves some open dates and a lot of people trying to get booked. So in a way, it helps if you're lucky enough to contact them at the right time. She tells me that a couple of SAMs had just dropped off their cards the day before she was getting her calendar book out to do some booking. So she put them on the list. They were lucky and happened to pop in at just the right time. She adds that making follow-up calls every couple of months to ask if she is booking yet, or when she is going to be booking again, is a good idea. Don't overdo it, though. One musician was messaging her at least once a week. That became annoying and it was too much. She said that once a month would be okay, but not more than that. "Following up is important" were her exact words.

I ask her, "What would you like the follow-up message to say?" Her first response is that sometimes the musician just sends their sales pitch again. In a mock hypothetical conversation type of way, she asks, "Did you even read my response? Do you realize you are talking to the same person?" She and I bounce back and forth on this topic and it becomes clear that she gets annoyed when someone isn't in a conversation with her. Let me explain it like this. A musician sent her a sales pitch query letter and she responded by saying, our calendar is full right now but check back in a couple of months when I'm doing more bookings. Then the musician followed up two months later by sending the same sales pitch query letter, instead of continuing the conversation with her. According to her, asking something like, "Did you like my promo video?" would have been a more appropriate follow-up. She prefers if someone initiates a follow-up by asking her, "Are you doing any booking or do you have any openings on your schedule right now?" or telling her about some of the places they have been playing. She expresses that she likes that one because she can see that they are out working and playing gigs.

We chat briefly about bad attitudes. Some musicians have reached out to her and then not followed up, or followed up once in a negative kind of way. Evidently, they have an attitude about not getting booked right away. She tells me she has new musicians asking her to play all the time and she's not going to chase down people that have a negative attitude.

She received a sales pitch from one musician who said, "Hi. I want to play there. Here's my video." Then she received a sales pitch from another musician and it had a little more information, like...

- This is the kind of music I play.

- This is how long I have been playing.

- These are some places I have played before.

She asks, "Which is going to catch my interest faster? Obviously, the one with more information."

She doesn't require that, or anything else, but it is helpful when she has many different people trying to get gigs at the brewery at the same time.

Tara tells me a story about one time when she had to make a fairly awkward phone call. When she took over booking the calendar at the brewery, she saw a couple of names that she didn't know. She wanted to learn about the acts, and she went down the list and looked each musician or band up on the internet. She found one of the duos that they had booked and learned that one of the two members had died. She had to call the other member and ask him if he was still going to come to play because they were on the calendar. The surviving member decided to come to play solo and so they rebooked him several times as a SAM.

As Tara and I are winding down our discussion the owner, Bryan Hackman, arrives, so I ask him to join the conversation. Bryan is the owner, founder, and brewer at Cotee River Brewing. He opened the brewery four and half years ago and has hired Solo Acoustic Musicians from the beginning. Bryan handled the music calendar for the first three years, with a little help from a couple of employees who no longer work at the brewery, so he passed on the calendar duties to Tara.

Bryan made sure to include a stage for music during the construction phase of the brewery. The stage is located in the front corner and people walking by can see the musicians through the windows. Brian tells me he has a love for music in general and when he was planning the brewery, he wanted to incorporate live music into his taproom. He tells me he chose the corner in hopes that the music would project really well across the whole room. He likes the idea of having musicians create art and fostering the environment of creating things just like he creates beer.

Bryan tells me that he really likes it when the musicians interact with the customers. He thinks it's fun and engaging them makes them more interested in being in the brewery. He says not every musician does it, but he thinks it's cool to see the audience give feedback and get into the music.

Bryan offers up some advice for SAMs who approach him for a gig. He says that whether it's just audio or video, he doesn't like when they send him music to listen to that has a lot of background noise. He thinks that Solo Acoustic Musicians should prepare their promo materials in private and not while they are playing a gig. He also adds that musicians shouldn't get discouraged if a venue doesn't jump on booking them right away. He tells me that he does keep all the business cards and information that musicians drop off or send to him or Tara. He says that when there's a lineup change, he goes through his files and may give them a call.

On my ride home I relax and listen to some instrumental acoustic music. I can admit that I am learning from these interviews and enjoying the conversations that I am having. Gaining so much knowledge and perspective of the other side of the gig transaction is eye-opening. I have been booking my own gigs for a long time and I am sure at some point I thought I knew everything, but this interview is proof that I still have work to do and things to learn to be the best Solo Acoustic Musician I can be.

I have always felt comfortable at this venue and in my communications with this client. Our conversations today were no different and I was very happy with the results. I am very grateful for Tara and Bryan taking time out of their day to share with me, and you, about how they see things with respect to booking musicians and managing a music program for a busy brewery in a thriving downtown. I always look forward to my gigs in their venue and will continue to play there as long as they will book me.

 # PROCRASTINATION

This part of the book took the longest to get finished by far. But seriously, folks, it was indeed hard to get started and hard to keep coming back to after every time I was distracted. I found it too easy to take breaks and wander off to do something else around the house like laundry. Making excuses to be irresponsible is a strong temptation and it's very easy to give in to it time after time. To be honest there were times that I thought I would never finish this chapter or this book because of my inability to stay focused on the task at hand.

Similarly, when it comes to booking gigs and initiating contact with a venue representative, I am a master at making excuses to put off the phone call or email for another time. I will tell myself it's lunchtime and they are busy. Or I will convince myself that since it's rainy, they are probably not in the mood to get a phone call from a musician. I have perfected a self-dialogue and it's kind of like a dance between the positive and negative voices in my head. It can either lead to me doing something productive or taking a nap. It never seems to matter that I always feel good after I do something and make forward progress. I still have to go through this inner fight to get things moving in the right direction.

It can be scary to call a complete stranger and ask them for money to play my music in their venue. I can work myself up and talk myself out of even getting started. Finding reasons why it would be better to put it off until tomorrow almost always seems easier than doing something about it. All of this is based on fear. The fear of rejection and the fear of failure are a big deal in sales, and that's what I am doing when I cold call a venue and ask for the entertainment director.

I have had to develop a little bit of a pep talk to get myself in the "zone" to make a call. It helps to remind myself that I have had success in the past when I make calls to book gigs. I tell myself that my product is good, that I am good at playing guitar and singing. I know my promo video is good and I know that people like it when I send it to them in an email. Still, I find myself in a position where I am lacking confidence and allow myself to fall into the trap of procrastination. I'll be right back. I have to go flip the clothes from the washer to the dryer.

And two hours later I finally find myself back at my computer typing about procrastination. But once again I find myself distracted by a phone call... and a snack... and, well, you get the idea.

Sometimes it seems so easy to put off the work it takes to keep my calendar full. I always come around and get to it, but I am trying to become more consistent with my business practices. Little things like adding follow-up notes to my calendar are helping me stay on task. When a manager says to get back to him on Monday and I make a small note on my calendar, I find that I follow up and often get that booking. It totally sucks when two weeks go by and I realize I was supposed to follow up a week and a half ago.

Has anybody ever said this to you? "What's the worst that could happen? They say no." Well, it's true. The opposite is true as well, because they could say yes. Procrastination is a self-imposed trap of helplessness and fear that should not exist. If you want to make one hundred sales calls trying to get gigs, then the best thing to do is to make the first one. The realization that some will say no and some will say yes should help conquer procrastination because it should alleviate the fear of rejection and the pressure of making a sale. I always feel better after I do something. Even if I don't see good results right away, I still feel better because I did something about it. And when I do book a gig and start a working relationship with a new client, I feel great.

Most artists, you know, spend their entire lives learning how to play music and write songs, and they don't really know how the music business works.
—Moby

As a musician, I deal with a lot of stereotypes. Other people often say or think musicians are overly emotional, flaky, or disorganized. I already deal with a lot of inner struggle coming from getting on stage in front of people over and over. Some people are nice and like my music, and some people are not nice and don't like my music. It is a difficult challenge to separate music from business. But both of them bring a fair amount of fear of rejection and fear of failure to deal with. Every night that I get on stage, I have a different group of strangers in front of me, and every time I make a phone call or send an email, I am contacting a different stranger. Some of them will like me and we will hit it off and work together for years to come and some of them will instantly reject my demo promo video and sales pitch.

I know all too well how easy it is to put off a follow-up phone call and go to the beach. I can offer examples of spending months and even years following up with someone and finally booking a gig. I can also relate examples of doing the same thing only to never get a gig at those venues. I have been persistent in the past and I have talked about the good business practices that I have shown before. I am being brutally honest here when I share with you that I am not perfect, and I do find myself falling into the procrastination trap sometimes. Convincing myself to make the call because I know that I will feel better afterward is a daily occurrence in my life. There are times when I have a good laugh at my own expense because I will build things up in my head and try to avoid doing the work and making the call, only to finally force myself to call the bar... and then be told the person is gone for the day. It's hilarious and unnecessary.

There are a lot of clichéd motivational sayings out there like "Just Do It." All of them apply to breaking the habit of putting things off. No one is going to book your calendar full of gigs for you, so you have to get over the hurdle and make it happen. You will always feel better by doing something about it. So what if one spot doesn't book you? If you gave it your best effort, you can be happy knowing that you did your part. Move on down the list of venues and get after it. Keep going and don't quit. Try to critique yourself, develop your sales pitch, and think of ways to improve your chances of getting gigs.

I talk to and email my sales pitch to so many different people, and I have to remember that not all of them are going to like talking to me or watching my promo video. Some of the people who are managing a venue's calendar are not nice people either, and they can project that negative attitude onto me in the way they respond to my sales pitch. It takes a tough person to deal with all the rejections that are inevitable in selling yourself and your musical product.

By the way, I have been fighting with myself the whole time I have been typing this chapter because part of me has been trying to convince the other part to stop typing and go the 7/11 and get some snacks. This book won't type itself, is what I keep saying to myself. I think I will stop right now, but only so I can force myself to make five sales calls to venues and hopefully, I will book a gig and land a new client.

If you take this section of the book and combine it with By the Numbers and Being a Chameleon, then you should get some work done on your calendar.

 # REJECTION

This is not a fun topic to talk about but it is an inevitable reality, so I thought it was appropriate to discuss it. I hope you are prepared for rejection.

Rejection is a negative word, and it affects our lives on every level. You can ask someone out on a date and they can say no. You can ask a friend to go do something fun and they can say no. You could ask someone for money or apply for a loan at the bank and they could say no. You could ask someone for a job or a gig and they could say no. You could play your guitar and sing in front of a group of people, and they could ignore you. It's just part of life to deal with rejection.

So why am I talking to you about rejection in a book about playing guitar and singing for a living as a Solo Acoustic Musician? Well, I think it's necessary to remind you that some people just aren't going to like you. They're not going to book you, and they may not even want to talk to you. They're just not going to like you. Yeah, I said that part twice, because it's important that it sinks in. We can't take it personally, and by that I mean you can't take it personally, because it won't be good for you.

I'm going to tell you a story now about a recent gig I played that didn't go so well, but I'm going to set it up by telling you how I got the gig. Over the last ten years, I have played at two locations of a restaurant chain that has four locations. Those two locations stopped having live music and the other two locations started hiring Solo Acoustic Musicians.

I wasn't really aware of this until one night back in August — it's December as I'm typing this — when a guy walked by, dropped his card in my tip can, and said to call him. I knew he was a bartender at one of their other locations. We had worked together for a few years and I always enjoyed working with him. He had always been enthusiastic about me playing there and used to tell me that he liked my music. I was pretty stoked at the end of the night when I was pulling my tip money out and there was a card for me to call.

I figured we were probably on the same schedule because he was a bartender, and when I got home at 11 PM, I called him and we talked for half an hour. He told me he had moved up in the company and was a manager and was in charge of booking the entertainment at this other location. He was very excited to tell me that he wanted to book me there because he enjoyed my music, and he thought I would be great for the other location.

This was awesome! What a great stroke of luck. I'm always chasing after gigs and trying to book gigs and here one just fell in my lap. I had done the work to get it, but he just happened to come to dinner with his girlfriend at the place I was playing on a rare Saturday night off. He saw me and thought, I have to book Michael at my location. I was surprised that I was going to get an opportunity to play in this other venue.

There are peaks and valleys in anything and that is especially true for the music business. It is very inconsistent. But if you are wise, you can let those downs really bring you to another level of your personality.
—Bryan White

Over the next couple of days, we texted back and forth, and then I went down to the restaurant on my way to another gig and stopped in to see him. He showed me where the setup spot was and grabbed his calendar. We booked a couple of dates. The stage area is completely outside, and they do not have an indoor spot so, unfortunately, I replaced the December date with a guaranteed gig. He was very cool about it, and it was not a problem. Then in late November came the first time I was going to play there and when I arrived, he wasn't there. I asked for the manager on duty and met a nice gentleman who showed me where to set up.

As I was setting up, another guy came over to talk to me and he had a pompous attitude. I don't know any other way to say this; he was a jerk. He proceeded to tell me he was now in charge of booking the live music and he had worked at such-and-such place and another place. His body language and his tone of voice, while he was talking to me, were very condescending and very know-it-all. I continued setting up and nodded and smiled while listening to him talk. I went over to my tip can where I keep my business cards to get one out for him. I said, "Here's my business card and I hope you like what I do tonight. This is my first time playing at this location and I'd like to play here again."

Long story short, throughout the whole night I could tell this guy didn't like me at all. He was very, very not into what I was doing. I've been doing this for a while so I'm pretty good at reading people's body language and facial expressions to determine their approval. When I was done with the gig, I went inside to the bartender to order my meal which was part of my pay. Then I went back outside to finish packing up my gear for my loadout. While I was packing up, one of the waiters came up to me and handed me the money that I was to be paid. He said, "The manager has your card and we will see you around town."

I thought this was pretty funny because this was a coward's way of not dealing with the fact that he didn't like me. He just didn't want to talk to me at all and I kind of smiled and giggled inside.

I've been doing this for a long time, and I've gone through a management change before. It sucks when a new manager takes over and wants to get rid of all the musicians that have played there before him so he can bring in his friends. Clearly, this was what was going to happen because this guy had been booking musicians somewhere else before and probably had people he likes.

I made $176 in my tip can that night, which is quite a bit above average, and the audience enjoyed me so it kind of sucks that this manager guy had an attitude problem and didn't like me. It's not him that I'm performing for, and it's not him who should be judging me for the songs I pick or the way I play — the people having dinner are the audience. By the way, it's kind of a fancy place so I was wearing a nice button-up shirt and slacks, watching my volume, and doing a good job of talking to people in the audience in a certain way. My only recourse was to text the manager that I had known for a few years and let him know that it was very obvious the other guy didn't like me. I also thanked him for the gig and told him to stay in touch because I don't expect to hear from the other guy.

This was a pendulum swing from ultimate acceptance to complete rejection on every level. I went there with a great attitude and was looking forward to playing the gig. It's a well-paying gig with really good food to take home. But when

I got there, I was greeted by a negative attitude from a guy I'd never met before. The guy I knew and expected to see when I arrived wasn't there. But the performance went well and the customers seemed happy at the end of the night. So blah, blah, blah, whatever.

One other thing: after I packed up and I was at the bar waiting for my food, the manager walked by and said, "Oh, I sent a waiter out with your money. Did he pay you? 'Cause I was busy with a party out back. But yeah, we appreciate you. See you around," and walked away very dismissively.

He was lying to me. He had told the waiter to make sure to tell me that he had my card, and that let me know that he had plenty of time to do it himself. By the way, there wasn't a party out back either. Also, I was paid in cash which means he had to take the time to count the money. And the cash was another weird red flag because, in all my years of working with this company and playing at their other locations, they had always paid by check. They also required me to fill out a tax form. Basically, it was not professional on his part.

I'm just trying to convey to you that I didn't take that rejection personally; it just motivated me to make some more phone calls to find more places to play. It didn't take long, either, because the next night I was at a gig and somebody walked up to me and said, "Hi, I own such-and-such restaurant and I'd like to hire you to play music. Do you have a card?" I gave them my card and we talked a couple of days later. They did indeed book me to play music at their place.

I guess there's probably a moral in this story. I'm not exactly sure what it is, but there are probably a lot of the clichéd uplifting posters I mentioned before that could apply to the situation. Things like...

"Keep your head up!"

"Don't quit!"

"Things are going to work out!"

All I know is, I knew what was happening and they treated me like I was stupid and didn't get it. I never let that get me down. I just came home and ate my salmon with Brussels sprouts. Then a couple of days later it all worked out for me with a brand-new venue that paid $50 more for the same amount of time, and so far that new venue is going really well.

Sometimes rejection is just part of the lifestyle or part of the job of being a Solo Acoustic Musician. Some people will sit down in front of you and then complain to the waiter or the manager that you're too loud or they don't like your songs. They're going to reject you. Don't let it turn you into a sour person. Just smile, play a happy song, and wait ten or fifteen minutes; they'll leave, and another group of people will sit down, clap for every single song you do and tip you in $20 bills. But if you let the table that complained about you and rejected you change your attitude and put you in a bad place, then when the next group comes in, they won't like you 'cause you'll be so negative that you won't play happy songs. In SAM 1, I talked about how a smile can change a situation. When dealing with rejection, a smile can definitely change your own personal attitude and even affect a whole room full of strangers in a gig situation.

How does this apply to booking gigs? You might be rejected right away in a phone call or an email, but you can't let it put you in a negative space. In this book, a few times, I have used the phrase "by the numbers" and that one rejection should motivate you to make five more phone calls or five more emails to find new venues. What you have to realize is that rejection is actually good, because that's probably not somebody you want to work with anyhow and now you have eliminated them from the list. Sometimes with the way technology is now, people will just ghost a conversation, meaning they won't respond at all for months or even years. So you can eliminate them from the list of people you need to call. If you have one hundred people or five hundred venues on your list, then just keep calling people you've never talked to before. But don't let previous rejections dictate your attitude, the way you're feeling about the next conversation or the crowd in front of you on the next gig, because then you only project negativity and insecurity.

You have to find a way to allow yourself to grow stronger by the rejection of someone else. That will spur you to make the next phone call and gain the acceptance of a new person, which will balance the equation. Then you can pat yourself on the back for dealing with rejection and moving forward to a positive outcome.

Believe it or not, not everybody likes my books or sends me nice emails or comments on social media. Although I may get a hundred nice comments, then somebody will say some really not nice things to me. It doesn't make much sense, because all I did was write a book trying to tell people what I knew about a subject. I have had to do some soul-searching to realize that the person being less than nice to me is probably unhappy with themselves and projecting it onto me. People have called me names. People have said my books are stupid, and people have said worse things. I just block them from my phone, email, or social media and I move on. I hi-five all the people that say nice things to me and I am truly grateful for their kind words.

It's like that in sales too. If you live in a town that only has three bars or restaurants that have live music, and two of the owners are jerks, then it's going to be a tough road to becoming a full-time musician. But if you can get yourself to a larger city or an area with a more dense population that has more places to play, you can make a hundred phone calls over a few months' time. You'll probably find yourself quite busy. Just don't give up. Always remember rejection is just part of the process, and don't take it personally because it happens to all of us. I have over thirty years of gigs, I am writing a series of books on the subject, and my sales pitch still gets rejected. I understand that not everyone is going to like me or my music and I keep moving forward with my life anyway.

The rejections are the opposite of the acceptance and hopefully, they'll make you appreciate the people who like you even more. Appreciate the people you like working with and remember you are always allowed to reject somebody who doesn't treat you well because it does go both ways. Some of these things are hard to not be emotional about or get caught up in, but if you remember some of the things I have said here, it will hopefully make it easier to navigate a situation where you're being rejected even without it being overt. As I said, I could tell all night from that one person's body language and the way he talked to me that he didn't like me from the moment he met me. I didn't let it get me upset, I played my gig the way I always do, I made good tips and I had fun.

Despite everything, I kept my cool and I was nice to everybody. I stayed in touch with the manager who booked me, whom I've known for several years, and who has given me the contact information of the manager at the fourth location where I've never played. I'm currently talking with her about playing at her venue. He also told me that another manager from a spot where I used to play is talking about having music again, so I contacted him. I know I'm on the shortlist for when they bring music back. Don't let a little rejection take you out of the game, take you out of your own head, or get you off-track. Stay focused on your mission. Understand it's going to happen, and the only thing you can control is how you react to it and how you move forward the next day.

Remember times when you've been accepted. Remember times when you made the cut and someone said yes. Think of all the people who like you and support you. Give yourself credit for trying. You took a risk by trying to book a gig — good for you. Remind yourself that you can handle rejection.

 **ATTITUDE**

Keeping a positive attitude can be a challenge when we are facing constant rejection and criticism. Sometimes it's hard to pick up the phone, make a call, and give a sales pitch to get a gig. Sometimes I just don't feel like it, but when I force myself to do it, that gets me in the mood or in the groove. Sometimes I really feel like it and I call and it goes great and sometimes I really feel like making the phone calls and I call and it goes badly and my whole mood changes. Pumping myself up before I make the phone call or send the email gets me into the Vortex of projecting confidence and an attitude of yes, I am good enough. I am awesome. I am deserving. I am good at guitar. I am good at singing. I am going to be on time. I am going to get this gig.

To be honest, I don't think that the type of thing I'm writing right now is forgotten when it comes to sales, but I also don't think a lot of musicians consider themselves salespeople. Even if you had jobs in sales or worked in a mall or a restaurant or even as a bartender, and now you're a full-time musician, you might not correlate those and realize that you are a salesperson.

You are running your own business, so that makes you an owner and an entrepreneur. You are providing a service; that makes you a worker, and that means you have to be good at your craft, which is playing an instrument and singing a song. You are also a marketing executive in charge of promoting where you're going to be and when you're going to be there. You have to plan and prepare for how you are going to sell yourself to the audience. On social media and with flyers in the venues, you will be selling yourself to customers. Customers are possible fans as well as venues. On top of that, you're in charge of some form of accounting or bookkeeping or hourly pay rates or something that involves communicating with a tax person at the end of the year.

How many more hats can we wear? You are also the roadie who loads the gear in and out. You also set up the gear and break it down. You are your own manager, your own business manager, and you are a booking agent for yourself. There are all these other skills you have to have in order to be successful that have nothing to do with playing your instrument, playing the guitar, and singing. I can sit on my couch and play guitar and sing all day. I could go down to the beach and sit on a bench and play my guitar and sing all day, but then I'd better have some other way of paying the rent. If I want to be successful in my job of playing my guitar and singing all the time, then I have to get good at some of these other things too.

To be honest I don't like some of the other parts of the job. I'm kind of good at some of them, mostly because I've been doing it for so long. I'm just kind of comfortable with it all and I feel confident that I play the guitar well and sing well. Also, I really enjoy playing my guitar and singing, so it just kind of makes sense to me. I never had to force myself to sell my product and services because it just kind of happened naturally. It was what I wanted to do.

I believe in my product and services and that helps me tremendously in my sales. Since we're talking about attitude, the fact that I believe in my product and I believe in myself helps me have a pretty good attitude most of the time. Don't get me wrong, there are times I get a mad, bad attitude and feel bad afterward because it's not productive. There are quite a few venue representatives who are not a lot of fun to work with. It can be a struggle to keep a positive, happy attitude when someone else is projecting negativity toward us. Right now I'm talking about when I'm on the job, but it also happens in phone calls and even emails or text messages when you're trying to get the job. What I can say is, don't take it personally and just try to do your best. It is another good reason to play the numbers game because if you make a hundred phone calls and you find five people that are jerks who are not nice to you, I'm pretty sure you're going to find the opposite as well: ten people who are super nice to you. That's just the way it goes.

The probability that one hundred people would be mean jerks and treat you poorly is very slim. It's more likely that it would be five or ten people out of a hundred that are mean. Then on the opposite end of that spectrum would be five to ten that were super nice. In the middle would be eighty people, or 80% of the people that you call, who are going to be okay. Just in the middle. Sort of nice, sort of nonchalant, and sort of indifferent. The bulk of your success is going to come from dealing with those people and having a good attitude.

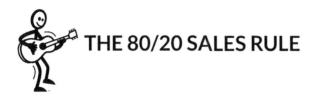# THE 80/20 SALES RULE

There are some different sales rules and principles and I'm going to talk about one of them right now. I'm no expert on these matters, and there are books out there on the subject. They are really easy to find with an internet search. But here's some basic information to get you started in understanding what I am referencing.

The Pareto Principle in business refers to the idea that 80 percent of a given business's profit typically comes from a mere 20 percent of its clientele. Business owners who subscribe to the "80/20 rule," as it's known, believe that the best way to maximize results is to focus the most marketing effort on that top 20 percent. This concept is important to understand because it can help you identify which initiatives to prioritize so you can make the most impact.

At its heart, the 80/20 rule simply underscores the importance of channeling your energy toward those aspects of your business — or life, sports activity, musical performance, blog, etc. — that get you the best results. However, it does not mean you should ignore the areas that are less successful. It's about prioritizing focus, tasks, and then solving problems that reveal themselves due to that focus.

Thinking this way can totally change your attitude. I have been playing a place every Monday since last February, and probably by the time this book comes out it will be more than a year. The staff is awesome; they show me a lot of love and treat me really well. I always show up there with a super happy-to-be-there attitude and positive energy, ready to smile and talk on the microphone with the audience. I give and get high fives and fist bumps from the employees. It always goes great, and I earn lots of tips. It's awesome and I have no struggle at all with my attitude on that gig. The management is great to work with and communicates well with the musicians. There is no pressure on me for anything and even dealing with weather obstacles is a breeze. Weather concerns are one of the most stressful parts of my job and in this venue, it is not stressful at all. I have a great attitude and confidence that things will go well every time on this gig.

When you're in the music business, everything is very personal, because you are invested in everything; there's a very deep, personal attachment to your music.
—Larry Mullen, Jr.

The opposite can be true, too: I could be at a place I've played for years and not really look forward to going there. Because it's just a blah situation. Not really fun, you know? But if I changed my attitude, I bet it would be better. If my attitude dictates how I feel and what happens, then of course it would be better. But when I show up walking slowly, lacking confidence, and am not really happy to be there, it might not go well. If I am just there because I need to make money to pay my bills, I might not have a good day. If I am projecting a bad or negative attitude, why would I expect a different outcome?

When I'm calling somebody to ask them to pay me to play a gig at their venue, I want to turn on my happy attitude and my awesome salesperson voice. Even though I'm probably sitting alone at home, whether it's in the morning, afternoon, or evening, I want to put a smile on my face and not act like it's a chore to make these phone calls. "Oh, my gosh, it's just a lot of work to do and I have to type things on my computer, and it's a drag on my energy." In reality, it's supposed to be, "Okay this is my mission. I'm going to call these people. I'm going to get gigs. They're going to give me money. They're going to be happy to hear from me. It's going to go awesome. Let's do it. Let's do it. Let's make these calls. Let's send out these emails. Let's go team Michael!"

We're going to get some gigs, then we're going to go to the venue, and we're going to be happy to be there. I'm going to set up, I'm going to smile, I'm going to sing happy songs. I'm going to play music. It is going to be great! Everybody's going to high-five and I'm going to make lots of tips. The venue is going to want me to come back and it's going to be great every time I play there. Let's make these phone calls. Let's make this sales call.

It is now 5:18 PM on a Sunday evening and I have just pumped myself up. I'm going to make a couple of phone calls and send some text messages and even some emails, so I'm going to stop typing. If I have pumped you up even a little bit, then put your bookmark in the book right now and get on your phone to make a call, text, or email. Send out a sales pitch and try to book a gig. That is my challenge to you. Pump yourself up with a positive attitude, because you are about to get a gig and it's going to be awesome!

Ready?

Set.

Go!

 **EMPLOYEE REQUESTS**

Once you get a gig and start playing a place regularly, you will begin to meet some of the employees. Make sure to take a second or two in passing and ask them what kind of music they like or who their favorite artist might be at the moment. These answers will be great leads on new cover songs to learn, in general, and especially for that venue. One thing is for sure, every time you play a venue the employees will be there. We always seem to focus on the members of the audience, and that is important, but don't forget the staff. This is just another small thing that adds to our longevity and success over the long haul when playing a place repeatedly.

I can remember quite a few times when I was having a conversation with someone who works in a venue where I play regularly and they would bring up a musician or artist that I'd never heard of before. It really helps to expand my horizons as a Solo Acoustic Musician to take note of their suggestions and look up the music. I have found several songs and artists that I'd never heard of, and now I really enjoy playing their music. Now I grant you, some suggestions are just not my cup of tea, but I try to keep an open mind. Lately, I have been even more accepting of strange ideas or requests, because I'm finding it fun to explore the music and myself musically.

Thinking this way actually led me to include "Piano Man" by Billy Joel in my songbook. Over the years many people have asked me to play that song and I always pointed to my guitar and said I'm on the wrong instrument, which I thought was a funny joke and a good response. But one of the bartenders I work with told me how much he really loved Billy Joel, and since I play there on a Saturday once a month I thought, well, it is a good Saturday night song because Billy Joel does sing the words "It's nine o'clock on a Saturday." Something kind of funny happened because now I really enjoy playing the song, and I enjoy singing it most of all. The song has come in handy at some other venues, where even if someone didn't request me to play "Piano Man," it's still a good sing-along to have in my repertoire.

I never thought of having platinum albums and winning awards. I just wanted to write songs and sing when I started out in the music business.
—*Randy Travis*

Recently I played my Sunday afternoon monthly spot at a place I have been playing for more than ten years. For the first three hours of a four-hour gig, I played songs that the bartender had never heard me do before. She is the owner's daughter and has been there for all these years and she said something to me about liking all the new songs. I know it works because she noticed and told me. On the same gig, when her replacement came in for what would be my last set of the day, I played a song for her too: one that she had requested the last time I was there. I didn't know the song at that time, but now I did so I surprised her with it. She couldn't believe I remembered her request from a month earlier and was very happy that I learned the song for her.

Sometimes I like to play obscure songs or deep cuts by famous artists or bands. A few months ago, I was at a place where I play once a month and I threw out an instrumental intro and flowed into a not-very-well-known Dave Matthews song. At that time I was very new to the venue, having only played there twice before, and I was cycling through a lot of songs so that I wasn't playing the same thing I played the first couple of times I was there. After I was done with this particular song, the bartender came out from behind the bar to tip me a five-dollar bill and told me that was her favorite band. When I took a break, I went over to get some iced tea and talk to her about that song. I told her that she must be a real fan if she knew that one, because that's not one of the popular songs. Then she showed me her arm where she had one of the Dave Matthews logos tattooed on her tricep. It was the fire dancer logo, and I recognized it right away. Now every time I'm there I throw in one or two Dave Matthews songs just for her. I think I've done ten so far without repeating any. She is blown away and tells me that nobody else who plays there does any Dave Matthews songs. The manager has also noticed that I learn what the employees like and that I throw songs in throughout my set lists just for them.

Another place I play regularly has a family-like staff; they have all been there for many years. So over time, I have asked all of them what they like to hear and learned songs for each employee. This has overlapped and helped me in other places. For one, I'm beefing up my overall song list and I'm keeping things fresh for myself. One of the bartenders there really loves '90s music. It's because of her age and when she grew up; it's the decade of music that influenced her in high school. So I really focused on learning a lot more '90s music.

This came in handy when one of the agents I work with, Jane Mckee, offered me a gig at a new venue. After the gig was booked and the details were sorted out she said to me, "Oh, and Michael here's a tip. They really like '90s music there. The owner and the manager are in their mid-thirties and they have repeatedly told me that they really like '90s music." My response was that I was well prepared for that situation and that I had really expanded my '90s music list within my overall songbook.

As you can see, it works out for me in more than one way to find out what the employees like. It's something you can do to help you keep a gig, and it can help you fill out your songbook in a way that prepares you to do well at new venues in the future. I have to admit there are some songs I really don't play anywhere else other than the place where I know that there is an employee who really likes that song or artist. Recently a customer in another venue requested one of those songs, and I happened to know it because I learned it for an employee who works somewhere else. If you haven't done it before, I hope you will try it the next time you're on a gig. Just start a conversation with someone who works at the venue you are playing and ask them, "So, what kind of music do you like?"

I have to add that it was kind of slow at my Monday evening gig last night, and I had a few minutes to talk with one of the bartenders. Usually, it's too busy to do much more than exchange a quick "hi, how are you?" but last night we got to hang out while I was on a break. He really likes Johnny Cash and I always throw one or two of those songs into my set for him. It's because of my asking him what he likes that I found "I've Been Everywhere," which has become one of my most well-received songs as well as one of my favorites to play. I have even added two original verses that I wrote for the song. One is based on my county and the towns in it, and the other is based on the state of Florida. I am thinking of adding up to three more verses based on the surrounding counties where I live and play. It goes over really well with my local audiences and even seems to be perceived as creative by visitors.

As we talked, he confided to me that after more than ten years of working at that venue five or six days a week (they have music seven days a week, and twice some days), none of the other musicians had ever asked him or any of the other employees what kind of music they liked. He added that it is one of the many reasons why I am one of their favorite musicians who play there. He also told me that they constantly get good customer reviews when I am there and that my approach of asking people what they like and what they want to hear has been working. I really appreciated the feedback; it made me feel good to know that I was doing something unique, that it was working, and that someone had taken notice. As I ended my break and walked back to the stage I smiled to myself and mentally patted myself on the back. Then I played another Johnny Cash song for TJ behind the bar.

I know this book is about getting a gig and booking a date on the calendar, and when I first started at that particular venue it was every other Monday. I truly believe part of the reason it quickly turned into every Monday was that I was asking the employees what kind of music they liked and taking requests. This particular venue has lots of regular customers, and I have developed somewhat of a following on Mondays but no matter what, the employees are always there, so they are the most consistent audience I am going to have. In a way, it's kind of like a secret message when I play some of the songs that are the favorites of the employees.

There are also two bartenders at the Tiki Bar in this location and I had never heard of Tyler Childers until I asked the other bartender, Katie, what kind of music she liked. I have since learned three of his songs and now he is one of my favorite musicians to listen to when I'm driving to a gig. That's an ever-evolving thing and it will change over time, but it is nice to know that when I throw one of those songs into my set that she knows I'm doing it just for her, because although Tyler Childers is growing in popularity I don't get requests from customers to play his songs.

So although this tactic didn't help me get the gig, it did help me turn it from every other week to weekly, and it also helps me keep the gig. If you don't know what kind of music, artists/bands, or genres the employees at your venue enjoy, I suggest you try to find out and play some of those songs during your gigs.

SPONSORS AND SPONSORSHIPS

I only have limited experience with being sponsored or having a certain kind of endorsement. I am going to explain my thoughts on the subject in the hope that it can help you understand more than you did before while giving you a spark of inspiration to go beyond what I have to say on the subject.

Yuengling beer is the USA's oldest active brewery. Light Lager is the main beer they make and sell. Here is their pitch from an internet search:

"An exceptional brew that appeals to consumers who don't want to sacrifice character for a low-calorie, low-carb light beer."

I did that search to make sure I spelled their name correctly because it was around 2005 when I was sponsored by them, which was a long time ago. Here are the details of what the "sponsorship" entailed.

The only contact I had with the actual company and headquarters in Pennsylvania was one phone call, followed by a letter in the mail from them, to give me what I needed to operate as an endorsed Yuengling representative. I was able to use this letter at any bar or restaurant to get all the "free" Yuengling beer I wanted. It also gave me permission to give away their brand-labeled gear, which I would procure from distributorships on a local level. The beer distributor is the one who delivers the beer to all the stores, bars, restaurants, etc. Back then these companies were under two basic umbrellas. One side was Miller and the other side was Budweiser. Yuengling was under the Miller company umbrella when it came to its affiliation with the county-level local beer distributorship.

I called and set up a meeting with the boss of the distributor so I could start promoting their beer. With my letter in hand and a plan to do a chugging contest, complete with a chugging song, I was able to get T-shirts to give away. I was given boxes of gear: shirts, hats, stickers, etc. Whatever swag the distributor had lying around and wanted to get out of their warehouse was put in my van. They also made me some promotional materials with a 50/50 ratio logo split. Half of the signs had my logo or picture, and the other half was the Yuengling logo. I was given a banner that was 3' x 6' or something like that. I could hang it up behind me or wrap it around the front of my merchandise table. The main point was advertising. I was never paid money by Yuengling or any other beer company, but I was given free promotional materials, swag to give away, and, you guessed it — free beer!

The "music industry" is not a term I use.
I tend to concentrate on music, and the
music business is something different.
—Mark Knopfler

There are several reasons that this was cool, and there are many levels of sponsorships or endorsement deals out there. What did it do for me? In my mind, it attached me to a brand. Having my name associated with a larger company makes me look cool. The people in the audience don't know the level of the deal or the details of my arrangement. All they see is my name, logo, or face next to a brand logo in my promotions. I was able to add a great crowd interaction trigger to my show. I was allowed to give away free beer to people at my gigs. By giving away the company T-shirts and other swag, I was able to engage the audience and add fun to my show.

The company spends a certain amount of money every year printing up these items and sending them to distributorships all over the country on a nationwide, regional, state, or county level. The distributor then has this stuff in their warehouse taking up space. They provide these items to stores, bars, restaurants, etc. Have you ever been somewhere like a tiki bar and out of nowhere the "Bud Girls" just show up and give away hats, necklaces, and koozies? Have you ever seen the amount of plastic green necklaces that beer and liquor companies put out there in the crowds on St. Patrick's Day? Have you ever been to a sporting event and seen someone throwing or shooting T-shirts up into the stands? Well, that is what I was doing at my shows. I was giving stuff away to audience members and bar customers in an attempt to engage the crowd.

It was a lot of fun. It was different and made me stand out. The venues I played liked that I was selling beer and pushing a product. As I said, I was never paid any money directly but it added to my persona and gave me added promotional materials for free. Whenever I played in a different state or county, I would call ahead and send my art examples to a distributor via email. I would coordinate the shipment of gear to be at the bar when I arrived in that town. It was extra work, but it was fun as well.

I have seen local bands and even Solo Acoustic Musicians team up with a local brewery to make a beer that is available in cans. This product could be a limited run and used for a charity fundraiser or some other special reason like a song/CD release. I admit that it looks cool to see your logo or picture on a beer can. The big thing, though, is the brand association that you get on all of the promotional materials. Operating like this on a small local level can be really cool.

I would love to have a sponsorship or endorsement from an instrument company like Martin or Taylor. (Hint hint...) That is probably a pipe dream for me but what is totally possible in my mind is something local. I could work with a smaller music store or something like that. In Tampa Bay, we have several companies that pop into mind right away. Gator Cases, Luna Guitars, and Dean Guitars are all headquartered here. We also have Sam Ash, Guitar Center, as well as other music stores that are not worldwide/national brands. I could probably work with any of these companies if I could give them a reason to be involved with my brand.

I could do a special fundraising concert or support a cause that would be helpful to my community. I could probably get any local company to be on the team if it was for the good of the people. If I was raising and donating money to the local community garden project, I am sure I could get a group of businesses to help me. A local brewery could supply a keg; shops (stores, spas, restaurants, golf courses) could give away prizes ($25 gift card, dinner for two, a massage, a round of golf) or packages for a silent auction; adding a 50/50 raffle would be cool; and since I live where I live, I bet I could get a beach hotel to put up a 1-2 night stay as a big prize. All of these partnerships could develop into an annual event associated with my brand. Even if I raise $1000 every year for the community garden, it would be a successful event and worth the effort.

When a musician, athlete, or celebrity gets into an endorsement/sponsorship agreement there are benefits. Of course, we all want to be paid millions of dollars to say how awesome a product or service is, but aligning oneself with a local company is just as beneficial for a musician like me. It's brand affiliation and company association that can help get people to take an interest in my products and services.

There is some psychology involved here. Let's say you can get a company to team up with you for some reason — you are now greater than yourself alone. It doesn't have to be a big company, either. It could be Adam's Accounting and Larry's Lawn Service who are your sponsors. The fact that these people believe in you and back you in some way lets other people know that you are worth investing in on some level. Even if it's "just for show," other people don't know that. Now, I am not telling you to lie or trick people. All I am saying is that people, in general, might assume Adam and Larry are paying you money to put their logos on your social media posts, flyers, and your website.

Maybe they are paying you a little bit of money and maybe they are not. Maybe Adam is doing your taxes and Larry is cutting your grass. In trade for these, you are putting their logo on everything you do in your music career and telling people that you like their companies. What do people see? They see Adam and Larry's companies as people who support you and believe in your musical abilities. If someone else thinks you are good and worth paying attention to, maybe they will check you out too. It can help you gain interest from people who might have never given you a chance.

Is there a local company of any kind that you really like? A favorite company or brand in your town that you would be proud to say you were associated with? Well, you could talk to the owner or manager about some kind of mutual situation where you cross-promote each other. What if you offer to play an annual company party in trade for a service? As part of the deal, you could add that you want permission to add their logo to your promotional materials. You could even add a tagline like, "Brought to you by (for example) Larry's Lawn Service." If someone asks you about your deal or affiliation with Larry's, you can answer them in an honest and yet vague way that protects your private business, something like, "Larry really likes to hear me play my songs and supports my musical endeavors." This is true and not specific to anything you and Larry agree to privately.

There are many opportunities out there to build a team of sponsors, and each one of them can have a different effect on your life and career. Of course, I wish you the best in landing a traditional corporate sponsorship, but don't be afraid or reluctant to build your network of businesses on a local level. I think you might just find that some other doors you weren't aware of at the time could open, providing other opportunities for you as well.

If you are a guitar teacher in a local music store, I think you should be allowed to include their logo on your promotional materials. You can ask them for permission and explain that you are loyal to their brand and want other musicians to know about their store. Tell them that you know lots of the local musicians in your area, and you know that they all see your social media posts about where you are playing. By adding the store logo to those flyers, you would be advertising for them as well. Doing this will make you look cool because other musicians will want to be allowed to put a music store logo on their flyers. If you have a good enough sales pitch, maybe you can negotiate a pack of strings once a month for payment of promotional advertising.

Sponsorships aren't always about greed, money, or things. Sometimes it's about alignment and association to further your brand in a direction that helps your public image develop to a new level. Building your perceived value can enhance parts of your music career. You could gain fans, it could lead to a pay raise on some gigs, and people might put more trust in your product. In my case, the Yuengling experience definitely added energy to my stage show because of audience participation and interaction.

Think outside of the conventional box and see what you can come up with. Ask a graphic artist to make you some cool flyers every now and then in exchange for putting their logo on your websites. Trade for an oil change agreement with a local car dealership. If I had the Tampa Dodge dealer's logo on my website, that would be pretty cool. It would help me tremendously to network and meet a manager or owner of the dealership. Look at your contacts and think about the six degrees of separation between you and someone who can make a decision and a deal. You might be surprised at how quickly you can get to an answer with a little effort.

Good luck with finding your future sponsors.

 **RED ROCKS**

I know this third book in the series is about booking a gig but in each of the previous books, I added some life stories and I'd like to do the same right now. I thought about this experience the other day when I was noodling around on the parlor guitar that I keep on the couch. So I went to my bedroom and pulled out a box of old pictures. After shuffling through them, I found a series of pictures of me playing guitar on the stage at Red Rocks.

Back in the late '90s, I was living in Colorado and one day I decided to go for a drive. I left the house in my navy blue 1972 VW squareback. If you don't know the model, it's a station wagon-type car with an engine in the back under the floor. I was kind of a hippie back then and eventually upgraded to a VW bus. I had a lot of adventures in both vehicles.

On this particular day, I decided to pick up a friend and get on the highway and see what we could see. Sometimes in life, it's fun to not have a destination or a plan. I don't specifically remember how we ended up at Red Rocks Amphitheatre. Both of us had been there to see concerts in the past, and I think we just saw the big green sign for the exit and I hit the highway off-ramp. I don't know if people can still do this, but back then, when there wasn't a concert scheduled, you could drive all the way up the road to the top of the hill.

There we were, standing at the top of the seating area looking down into the Red Rocks Amphitheater. It was empty except for a few other people wandering around. I decided to grab my acoustic guitar from the car and hike down to the stage. My friend stayed at the top and took some pictures as he made his way down through the seating area. A total of twenty-four pictures from different spots from the top down to the stage. It was a complete roll of film, and I couldn't wait for them to be developed the next day.

I'm not sure what to call the seats, because they're kind of giant stone rows where people stand to watch the concert; it's not like the seating area of a typical indoor venue. It's a beautiful space and if you have never heard of it or seen it, look it up. Red Rocks is located in Morrison, Colorado, just outside of Denver.

It was a lot of fun to stand on that stage and play guitar and sing for about 20 minutes. It was a famous concert venue even then, but it has gone on to become an iconic place to see a concert or, if you're in a band, to play a concert. I know people that brag that they have been there for a concert, and I like to grin and remember that I've actually played a few songs on that stage. Here's something funny, though: a few other people had the same idea as us, of going there on a day when there wasn't a concert, and in some of the photos there's a group of four guys back to my left playing hacky sack on the stage. This reminds me of how sometimes when I load in for a gig at a venue with a stage and there will be kids running around and jumping off it because there's no band, so it's just a platform.

We didn't really hang out for long, but we wandered around a little bit, just checking the place out because it's different when there aren't thousands of people there. We made it back to the top of the hill by the car, and it was time to go, so we hopped in the squareback... and it wouldn't start.

It had a manual transmission, so I put it in neutral and we started pushing the car down the hill. Then we jumped in and I popped the clutch. It started right up and off we went. Anyway, that's my story about playing guitar at Red Rocks Amphitheatre. I wasn't hired to be there, and my name wasn't on any tickets, advertisements, or posters, but I did play guitar on that stage. It's kind of fun to be able to say that.

 **AFTERWORD**

I truly believe there is a lot of information in this book that will help you get gigs. There are many books out there about the music business or the industry as a whole. They are all written from somebody's particular perspective, whether they're a musician or a producer, or even a record company executive. I have not found any books that actually go behind the curtain and talk to the people who run venues and hire musicians on a local level. It is my hope that this book offers a unique perspective and that you were able to gain some wisdom through the information that was shared with us in the interviews. I found uniqueness in each interview, as well as several common themes. My suggestion to you is to note the things that stood out to you and that you think could help you the next time you have a conversation with a venue representative about booking a gig. I was pleased that everyone I approached about sitting down to talk with me was so agreeable and honest. It genuinely seemed like they opened up and told me what they thought about Solo Acoustic Musicians.

It can seem that technology advances and changes the landscape of our mission as SAMs, but all of the old-school things still work, like having a conversation with a venue representative and knowing what to ask them and also how to answer their questions. In all my years of experience, I have had lots of conversations with the people who are managing the calendars, but I have never sat down and directly asked them a line of questions about the subject. I had fun learning about their side of the deal and I think there's a lot of good information within those conversations. I know it will help me make a few adjustments to my sales pitch and how I approach new clients. Right now, I am actively going through a database of venues and picking out the ones I want to contact about getting a gig. These will be potential new clients that I hope to turn into repeat clients. I am going to test my newly energized sales approach and I think I will see positive results. Reading back through these interviews pumps me up with the energy to go out and meet a whole new batch of potential clients to which I can sell myself and my music.

Again, a lot of this may seem like common sense but there are definitely some hidden gems in these talks with managers, owners, and agents. Even if you are a very experienced SAM this book might help you, because all of us can fall or slip into ruts very easily in any aspect of our career or lifestyle. I find that taking a new perspective on trying to get a gig can be refreshing and help renew my focus when it comes to hunting for new places to play. Even if only one small thing in this book helps me to land one new client that becomes a once-a-month gig on my calendar for the next year, it will totally be worth the time it took to prepare these pages. I may up my game by taking this renewed outlook out there into the world to find five new clients who book me once a month for years to come. In this case, I will be incredibly happy with myself for applying this information in a real-life scenario.

I will never understand why some venues respond to me and some don't respond at all, or just ignore me for a long time. I'll also never understand why a place I've been playing for several years will suddenly ghost me and quit booking me. I don't think any of us will ever truly know everything that happens on the venue side. At the end of the day, all I can do is try my best to communicate with the venue representative and keep my calendar full.

I wish all of you who have read this book the best in your music adventures and your interactions with the people who manage the calendars of the venues you approach. Good luck and happy gigs!

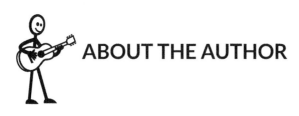

ABOUT THE AUTHOR

Michael Nichols has been a singer-songwriter and working musician for thirty years. He currently lives in the Tampa Bay area of Florida. Growing up singing in a church choir and the school chorus was a great beginning for his life in music. After trying several other instruments before putting his hands on a guitar, he didn't get into the drum set, piano, violin, or saxophone. Mr. Nichols started "gigging" for money when he was fourteen years old and has played music in almost every situation possible. After all these years of playing out, he has developed a playbook of the dos and don'ts of being a Solo Acoustic Musician. Michael is still playing almost three hundred gigs a year and staying busy in his community. As a Paul Harris Fellow involved with Rotary International, he has donated money and time to charitable activities over the years.

 # ACKNOWLEDGMENTS

First of all, I want to thank all the fans for sending in photos of the books or themselves with the books. It's always a surprise and makes me smile when I receive those messages and emails. Believe it or not, I had no idea I was going to write a second and third book after I wrote SAM 1. It is because of the response from all the nice people around the world who have taken an interest in reading SAM 1 that the other books exist.

I thank you for that overwhelming feeling of gratitude.

Secondly, I would like to thank the musicians who were kind enough to talk to me and be interviewed in SAM 2 as well as the managers, owners, and agents who sat down with me for this book. I learned a lot and I appreciate all of them taking time out of their day to share their experience and wisdom with us. SAM 2 and SAM 3 reach beyond my own perspective and it is because of these folks. Thanks to you all!

Lastly, I would like to give some props to the people behind the scenes. Phil has been the editor for all three books. He gets what I am trying to do and really helps clean up my mess. The publishing team at DartFrog Books has been crucial in getting these books across the finish line and I appreciate their hard work immensely. Gordon, Suanne, Mark, and Simona do an awesome job and these books would not exist without them. Thank you, Team Solo Acoustic Musician.

You can find links and merchandise on the website.

Solo Acoustic Musician: A Practical How-To Guide

Solo Acoustic Musician 2: New Tips, Stories, and SAM Interviews

soloacousticmusician.com

Printed in Great Britain
by Amazon

26788160R00142